Praise for
THE TRANSFORMATIVE POWER OF TEN MINUTES

"The experience of stress has become a major part of most, if not all, of our lives. Not surprisingly, ongoing stress has a major impact on our emotional and physical well-being, on our relationships with others, on our performance in school or work, and on our sense of contentment. Dr. Beth Kurland has written a very informative, reader-friendly book outlining a practical approach for managing stress and cultivating positive emotions. The strategies she proposes are realistic and ones we can all embrace. Dr. Kurland's appreciation of and empathy for the difficulties we all face in implementing lifestyle changes, as well as her encouragement for making these changes, are evident on every page of her impressive book. This book will serve as a wonderful resource to be read and re-read as we all strive to lead more resilient lives."

—*Robert Brooks, Ph.D.,* Faculty (part-time), Harvard Medical School
Co-author, *The Power of Resilience: Achieving Balance,*
Confidence, and Personal Strength in Your Life

"Dr. Kurland has mastered the art and science of using psychology for personal transformation. In a world where stress is a mainstay, Kurland eloquently lays out a path to making high impact behavioral changes to cultivate well-being. Her voice, worksheets, and every day examples provide us with just the right dose of inspiration that fits within even the busiest of schedules. This is a low investment, high return program that will be an asset to classrooms, therapy rooms, and everyone's bookshelf."

—*Dr. Kristen Lee, Ed.D., LICSW,* Behavioral Science Professor, Northeastern University
Author of *Reset: Make the Most of Your Stress,* Motivational Book of 2015 Winner

"Beth has put together such a well rounded resource on living mindfully, managing the day-to-day stresses of busy life and developing healthy habits. This is an easy-to-follow, clearly laid out path that will be of great benefit to any who are fortunate enough to take up its invitation. Bite-size, realistic tasks are offered to the reader that progressively build on each other and hold the potential to transform your life, from struggle to well-being and joy."

—*Kellie Edwards*
Psychologist & Mindfulness Teacher
www.Mindfulness4Mothers.com

"Despite all of the self-help books that are available today, almost none offer practically useful tools that can be used by the average reader, and even fewer are based on our knowledge of what actually works from scientific research. *The Transformative Power of Ten Minutes* is an exception to both. The advice and exercises provided in this book can be trusted because they come from work that has proven effective. And they can be used because Dr. Kurland has presented them in a way that pretty much anyone can understand and act on. Following the steps in this book is an excellent way to reduce your stress, improve your life, and help fight depression, anxiety, relationship problems, and the other difficulties we experience in today's world."

—*Paul Block, Ph.D.,* Clinical Psychologist, VP for consulting, OPEN MINDS

"As a physician of 18 years in a community primary care setting, I am keenly aware of the effects of stress on health and well-being, and am constantly looking for tools to benefit my patients. This book offers just that: practical tools to harness the benefits of mindfulness in order to help manage one's own overall health. This book is clear, accessible, and easy to implement through its daily exercises. I found my own shoulders relaxing as I read this book, and found myself benefitting from greater awareness of my stress and particularly like the many ways to reinforce positive neural connections through the exercises. It is a great read for anyone wanting to take charge of their own health and wellness."

—*Julie Crosson, M.D.,* Director of Communication Skills
Boston University School of Medicine, Internal Medicine Residency Department

"Dr. Kurland's words and encouragement offer all of us the opportunity to cultivate well-being. Using ten minutes a day, she shows how to completely transform our thinking and stress responses. With her gentle approach and easy to follow exercises, Beth paves the way for us all to incorporate these techniques into our daily lives. A powerful book that is a pleasure to read!"

—*Shari Engelbourg, M.Ed.*, Educator, 500-hr. Registered Yoga Teacher

"Help is here: Dr. Kurland does a beautiful job providing helpful, practical wisdom to help reduce stress and gain perspective. Whether you work your way through all eight weeks or simply keep going back to one exercise you find most helpful, Dr. Kurland becomes your own private mindfulness coach. Think of this book as roadside assistance for the stress of life. You are going to want to have both a physical paper copy in order to write inside and complete the insightful exercises she provides as well as an electronic copy so you can always have this book with you."

—*Rabbi Joseph B. Meszler,* Temple Sinai, Sharon, Massachusetts

"'I don't have time to be mindful!' We've heard about the impact that stress can have on our physical, psychological and social well-being. We've also heard that there are techniques we can use to help reduce that impact. Dr. Kurland provides an informative and interactive plan to learn these techniques and integrate them into each day. With useful information, paper and pencil activities and audio guidance, this book can be an extremely useful tool as we cultivate well-being and make the transformation from 'stressed out' to a place of personal wellness."

—*Carol Dolan, Ph.D.,* Clinical Associate Professor
Boston University School of Public Health

"*The Transformative Power of Ten Minutes* is one of the clearest guides I have come across to understand and develop a mindfulness practice. The writing is clear and easy to understand, incorporating a host of effective metaphors. The format provides the reader not only with a clear understanding, but also with well thought out daily exercises to move you into practicing the lessons, deepening your understanding, and having some early wins to fuel your practice. I love how many exercises are supported with an audio clip and worksheets. It is clear Beth Kurland wants her readers to practice the exercises and gain the benefits of being more mindful in their lives. Whether you are new to mindfulness or have an established practice, this is a valuable resource for all. Well done!"

—*Scott Orth,* Business Consultant and Resilience & Productivity Coach

The
TRANSFORMATIVE
POWER of
TEN MINUTES

The
TRANSFORMATIVE
POWER of
TEN MINUTES

An Eight Week Guide to Reducing Stress and Cultivating Well-Being

BETH KURLAND, Ph.D.

WELLBRIDGE BOOKS
An Imprint of SIX DEGREES PUBLISHING GROUP

ISBN: 978-1-942497-27-1
(eISBN: 978-1-942497-23-3)

Cover Design: Eve Siegel; evesiegeldesign.com

Publisher's Cataloging-in-Publication
(Provided by Quality Books, Inc.)

Kurland, Beth, author.
    The transformative power of ten minutes : an eight
week guide to reducing stress and cultivating well-being
/ Beth Kurland.
    pages cm
    Includes bibliographical references and index.
    LCCN 2016962306
    ISBN 978-1-942497-27-1 (alk. paper)
    ISBN 978-1-942497-23-3 (eBook)

    1. Stress management. 2. Stress (Psychology)
3. Relaxation. 4. Mindfulness (Psychology) 5. Stress
management--Popular works. 6. Self-help publications.
    I. Title.

RA785.K865 2017   155.9'042
                          QBI17-900013

Printed simultaneously in the United States of America, the United Kingdom and Australia

1   3   5   7   9   10   8   6   4   2

To Alan — for your infinite devotion.

*To Eve and Cindy — whose encouragement and enthusiasm
made this book a reality.*

To ALL of my amazing family — for your support and love.

*And to my fellow travelers on this path — that you may
discover greater ease and joy on your journey.*

CONTENTS

PREFACE & ACKNOWLEDGMENTS

IF I had to trace the origins of this book, it probably began in 1992 when I had the privilege of working with Dr. Robert Brooks, my supervisor during my psychology internship at McLean Hospital. I was greatly influenced by Dr. Brooks' work on resilience and his strength-based model for working with patients. Rather than just focusing on psychopathology, I learned how to identify patients' strengths and build resilience as a focus of treatment. In the twenty-three years since then, I have incorporated this into my work with patients, and have developed a strong interest in treating not only what is "wrong" when people come to see me, but also helping them to develop a strong sense of well-being and resilience in their lives.

In 2014, I was fortunate to take an online course with Dr. Clayton Cook (2014) entitled "Becoming a Resilient Person: The Science of Stress Management and Promoting Well-being." This course excited me because it was on a topic I am most passionate about and one which I had been teaching and practicing for years. The course sparked my interest in developing an eight week group in which I could pull together material from many areas of psychology, to help people learn concrete tools to promote greater well-being in a group setting, similar to what I had been doing individually with my patients over the years. Dr. Cook's course inspired the framework and structure for this group. As sometimes happens in life, for a variety of reasons I was unable to schedule this group as I had hoped. Reminding myself to call on my own resilience, and not give up on my goal, I decided to develop my program into a book that could reach a wide audience. Drawing from my years of clinical experience and knowledge of evidence-based practices, I began writing. During this time, I also had the good fortune of taking two other wonderful online courses, one with Dr. Ronald Siegel (2013) called "Mindfulness and Psychotherapy," and one with Dr. Rick Hanson (2015) entitled "The Foundations of Well-being." These courses also resonated strongly with my interests, and they became an inspiration for this book.

*   *   *

When I was raising my children, friends would often use the phrase "it takes a village," (from Hillary Clinton's book of that title) referring to the number of people involved in helping with the enormous task of child-rearing. I am reminded once again of that phrase as I reflect on the process of writing and publishing this book. There are so many people who have contributed, directly and indirectly, to this journey.

I want to acknowledge the tremendous support of Eve Siegel (my mother since adolescence) and Cindy Li (my sister), who have been there with me every step of the way, reading chapter after chapter and giving me the encouragement to continue writing because they believed this book was worth putting out into the world. Without their feedback and encouragement this book would have likely remained a partially written manuscript on my hard drive. Thank you to Cindy for fielding daily phone calls from me asking for input about one thing or another. It helps to have a sister who is both a best friend and a skilled psychologist. Also, a giant thank you goes out to Eve for the design of the book cover, and for helping to design all of the worksheets for this book.

I am so grateful to have such loving support from my entire family and extended family. A very special thank you to my husband, Alan, for always being there for me. Alan's calm and loving presence has been a great source of strength and refuge for me. The way that he so gracefully and calmly balances his life as a compassionate physician, loving father, devoted husband, and photographer extraordinaire, (to name a few of his many roles) continues to inspire me and leave me in awe. In addition to all of his emotional support throughout this process, and always—he has been invaluable in helping me with all of the technical aspects of things from my website to helping me edit all of the audios that go along with this book. Thanks to my father, Lewis Siegel, whom I admire greatly, who has been a wonderful teacher, role model and inspiration for me over all these years. Thanks to my two children who fill my life with joy, and who have taught me so much about resilience and perseverance. I am so thankful for my brother Mike Siegel, who has offered me so much support and friendship through the years. I am grateful to have such loving in-laws, Susan and Ray Kurland, who have been at the top of my cheering committee for this book, and for everything I do. Their support has meant so much to me. My extended family of sisters and brothers-in-laws, cousins, nephews and nieces, have enriched my life so deeply.

I want to acknowledge Allison Jones, whose exceptional editorial skills were so valuable to me in preparing the final draft of this book. I also want to offer a big thank you to Bruce Jones, who has helped me step out of my comfort zone in many ways, and has offered his expert advice on book marketing, website set-up, social media, and the technical aspects of things that I would never have known how to do on my own.

This book would truly not be possible without the incredible efforts of my publisher, Denise Williams. From our first interaction, and consistently throughout, Denise has demonstrated a caring, warmth and support, in addition to her expertise in all aspects of publishing, that have made this process truly delightful. I am most appreciative that she believed in this book and that we have had the opportunity to work together. It has been a true privilege and I cannot imagine a better publishing experience.

I want to express my deep appreciation to all of the people who have taken the time out of their busy lives to review my book: Robert Brooks, Kristen Lee, Carol Dolan, Kellie Edwards, Paul Block, Joseph Meszler, Julie Crosson, Shari Engelbourg, and Scott Orth.

A special thank you goes out to Paul Block, whose first reading of this book and feedback was instrumental in my going forward. I have always had the utmost respect for Paul's focus on evidence-based clinical work, and getting his blessing on my first manuscript meant a lot to me coming from someone I respect so highly.

I also would like to take another opportunity to acknowledge Bob Brooks, whose work I so greatly admire, and whose help and support along many phases of this journey have been invaluable. In addition, I would like to express my appreciation to Rick Hanson, Ron Siegel, and Clayton Cook, whose wonderful courses inspired some of the material in this book. Furthermore, I would like to acknowledge the inspirational work of Jon Kabat-Zinn, Daniel Goleman, Daniel Brown, Daniel Siegel, Barbara Fredrickson, Martin Seligman, and Sonya Lyubormirsky, among those above and many others, whose work has been monumental in the field of psychology.

There are so many teachers, mentors, therapists, mind-body practitioners, and friends that I would like to acknowledge—who have played an important role in my personal well-being. Thank you to my "circle of women"—Shari Engelbourg, Nadine Vantine-Kelley, Sara Dolinsky, and Cheryl Opper—who have been on this journey with me for the past 21 years. Thank you to Laureen Berkowitz and Elise Siegel, for your friendship and support, and to ALL of my friends who have enriched my life. A special thanks to Jessica Kahan for encouraging me with my writing, and to Paul Kolodzinski for our insightful poolside chats. I am also so grateful to Beverly Feldman, who has been an added part of our family since the birth of my daughter, for all of her support and devotion over the years.

Thanks to my bike friends Jack Gregory, Nancy Mollitor, Allison Jones and Jenna Koines, for their company, and for listening to the evolution of this book. Barbara Strassman, Lois Freedman, David Stern, Shelley Tanenbaum, Tony Tavares, Linda Mcgettigan and Alex McKinney have all contributed greatly to my mind-body health and wholeness, and I am truly grateful for my relationship with them over the years.

I also want to acknowledge Michael Goldberg and all of my colleagues at Child and Family Psychological Services with whom I have collaborated since 2001. I greatly respect each and every one of them and I have learned from their clinical expertise.

This book would not be complete without sending a heartfelt acknowledgment to all of my patients over the years with whom it has been a great privilege to work. They have allowed me to share in their deepest sorrows and joys as they have courageously faced life's challenges and taught me about the strength of the human spirit.

And last, I want to acknowledge my mother, who was my very first teacher, and gave me the secure foundation upon which I stand. I wish she could be here to share in the joy of my first book, but I know she is with me always.

INTRODUCTION

IF YOU HAVE PICKED UP THIS BOOK, you are probably wondering how 10 minutes a day could benefit you or, possibly even lead to significant changes in your life. In this fast-paced world where we often find ourselves taking on too much and feeling overwhelmed, the thought of setting aside an hour or more a day to make changes in our lives would likely feel daunting. But what if 10 minutes mattered? What if setting aside 10 minutes a day could change the way you react to stress and help you begin to experience more joy and ease in your life? Would you invest in that time for yourself? Similar to physical therapy, in which 10 minutes of daily exercises can help strengthen weak muscles and transform the way we move, the exercises in this book are designed to carry over into all aspects of your life and they can be continually practiced and reinforced as you go about your normal day.

Despite all the years we spend in school, and the many more years that we spend on this planet, we often are not taught how to navigate life's challenges. Even many well-meaning parents are unsure how to teach these important life skills to their children. As a result, most of us go through life without a road map. Yet life is inherently challenging, and being human means that we often face regular stressors, frequently daily ones. Being a clinical psychologist allows me to see firsthand and quite intimately the common struggles and suffering that we all face, that make up this shared humanity we call life.

Whether our stressors involve raising children, managing challenges in the work place, navigating intimate relationships, taking care of ailing parents, having too much to do and not enough time to do it, struggling with anxiety, depression, poor self-image, illness, feeling that stress has taken the joy out of our life, or any other multitude of issues, we often are left to manage on our own. When I was raising my children people often said things like "too bad kids don't come with an instruction manual." I think most of us could say that about life itself. This book is my attempt at that instruction manual.

But this book isn't just an instruction manual. It is the result of a very personal calling that began more than thirty years ago, and the insights I've gained along the way, both personally and professionally. At the beginning of this journey, back in my junior year of high school, I was grappling with profound grief after my mother died the previous year. At the same time, I took my first psychology class and became a "mentor" for a younger, middle school student. This student was struggling with many social pressures, anxiety, and a challenging home situation. In addition, a very close friend was suffering with severe depression after his own mother committed suicide. I knew even then that I wanted to help people, to somehow bring greater ease to people's lives and support them to feel less alone in their life struggles.

Directly after high school, I pursued a career in psychology and earned my doctorate, often letting life become my teacher, as well as some wonderful mentors, teachers, and therapists along the way. Someone once told me that we often teach others what we most need to learn ourselves. The double benefit of pursuing this path has been that I am able to first try out and benefit from all the tools and strategies that I later share with my patients. Now I have the opportunity to share them with you as well.

This book is about transforming stress and developing greater joy, ease, and overall well-being in your life. It does not offer a magic pill to make life's stressors disappear, because change, sadness, hardship, and challenges are inevitable parts of life. However, when we cultivate the inner resources to cope better and to become more resilient, we interrupt the cycle of chronic stress and make room for greater peace, joy, and gratitude in our lives.

I have selected and created for you a complete tool kit drawn from years of experience with evidence-based practices grounded in science and research, designed to bring about effective and positive change. This book can be thought of as a kind of "greatest hits" album, synthesizing and utilizing what I believe are some of the most fundamental and helpful skills from the fields of Cognitive-Behavioral Therapy, Mindfulness, Positive Psychology, and a field in psychology called Acceptance and Commitment Therapy. My goal in sharing this book is to give you practical tools and strategies that you can put into action in an immediate and lasting way, by making one small change every day over the course of eight weeks, and more. I have learned in my own life, and from the lives of my patients, that when we have the right tools, we are capable of not just surviving and getting by, but of transforming to a life of thriving and flourishing.

Unlike many other books, this guide offers short, daily exercises, with an accompanying audio component (look for the audio 🔊)) symbol adjacent to the weekly exercise numbers) and worksheets, to help integrate each of the skills into your life. Worksheets are included at the end of each weekly chapter. Additional copies of the worksheets and audios are available for free online by visiting my website BethKurland.com.

One of the skills you will learn in this book is mindfulness, a way of bringing our awareness to THIS moment in a nonjudgmental manner that allows us to observe our own experience. Mindfulness, which was an essential part of Buddhist meditation practices thousands of years ago, has become a mainstream skill taught throughout the country to children and adults alike, thanks to the efforts of modern science and neuroscience which have shown its effectiveness and benefits in many areas of our lives. Mindfulness offers a way to experience difficult emotions by observing them with an attitude of acceptance and non-judgment that helps keep us from being pulled in and swept away by these emotions. It also offers a way to appreciate the moment–to–moment joys of life that we so often miss when we are not paying attention.

If you are reading this book it is likely that you want to change some aspect of yourself or your life. So how do you change? What does it mean to change? If we are trying to change how we react to stress, how we wake up and experience the world each day, how we behave day in and day out, how we feel and how we think, we are talking about changing the neural pathways in our brains that are responsible for our reactions to daily events. In recent years, modern neuroscience has turned the notion of brain "plasticity" (the ability to change the brain) upside down. Once upon a time it was believed that after a certain age in youth, our brains were essentially formed, and that, as the old expression goes, "you can't teach an old dog new tricks." This is no longer believed to be the case. In fact, neuroscience has demonstrated in fascinating and repeated ways that we can rewire out brains at any age, and in much shorter amounts of time than were ever before believed (Begley, 2008).

Sharon Begley, in her book *Train Your Mind Change Your Brain* (Begley, 2008) illustrates through a review of fascinating scientific studies how the brain can be modified and rewired at any age in ways never before thought possible, leading to measurable physical changes in the structure and function of various parts of our brain. As one example of this kind of neuroplasticity, Dr. Herbert Benson, founder of the Benson-Henry Institute for Mind Body Medicine in Boston, describes a study in which just eight weeks of relaxation training (20 minutes a day) altered the activity of the participants' genes in dramatic ways (Benson & Proctor, 2010). This change in gene expression (whether certain genes are turned on or off) helps determine the state of a person's health and their risk factors for developing certain diseases. A recent article in *Scientific American* (Ricard, Lutz, & Davidson, 2014) reviewed the findings of research on the benefits of meditation and reported numerous studies showing significant positive changes in the brain structure of people who meditate, including changes at the molecular and genetic level. These kinds of findings have been exploding in recent scientific literature.

How To Use This Book

This book is all about increasing your awareness of where you are getting stuck in your life; learning new skills to bring about change; and practicing these skills to experience the results first hand. You will learn about the powerful connection between the mind and the body, and many of the exercises in this book use mind-body experiential strategies. In order to learn a new skill and make it part of our lives, neuroscience teaches us that we need to get as many neurons as possible to fire together in new ways, with enough repetition, that a new pathway can be laid down.

A commonly heard expression in the neuroscience field is "neurons that fire together, wire together," (a concept that originated in the work of psychologist Donald Hebb, considered one of the fathers of neuropsychology). Modern neuroscience compares rewiring the brain to going to the gym to build muscles. In order to get muscles to become stronger and bigger, we need to go to the gym regularly and do specific exercises that get those muscle fibers to fire in certain patterns. With enough repetition, change occurs. Something similar happens when we rewire our brains. We need to recruit new neural pathways, and we need those pathways to fire repeatedly, and with enough consistency in order to lay down lasting neural changes in the brain. This book is intended to help you make these changes, by offering you simple, daily exercises that will allow you to decrease stress and experience more positive emotions in your life. It also serves as your very own personal trainer, offering you a comprehensive program laid out for you to bring about results through daily practice.

When I talk with my patients about brain plasticity I use the analogy of a well-worn path in the woods. If we walk the same way day after day in the woods, a path becomes well worn. Every time you enter the woods, it becomes easier and easier to follow that path, until it becomes quite automatic. If we want to change a pattern of behavior or a habitual way of thinking, we need to create a new path in the woods. We need to walk this new path over and over. The more we do this, the better that pathway gets carved out, until a new behavior or way of thinking and being becomes much easier to engage in with less effort. (A word of caution: Some pathways can be more easily changed than others. For example, for those who have experienced significant traumas in their lives, while these exercises can still be very beneficial, it will be helpful and important to work with a skilled therapist who is trained in working with trauma to help promote healing and change.)

In the following chapters you will find a kind of tool kit, filled with everything you will need to help you make simple yet profound changes in your life. The inspiration for the structure and framework of this book grew out of an online course that I participated in, taught by Dr. Clay Cook (2014). The information is presented in a concise and concrete way to make it simple and easy to implement in a short amount of time.

In Week One you will become aware of the ways stress manifests in your life, the cost of this stress, and what you can do to interrupt the stress cycle. In Week Two you will examine what matters most to you in your life, and learn how focusing on what you most value can keep you motivated to work toward your goals and create a supportive road map for your journey. In Week Three, you will recognize how much of your life is spent thinking about the past and/or future, and see that to experience true peace and joy, you must learn to be present in the now. You will learn simple mindfulness tools to do this. In Week Four, you will learn the power of your thoughts and how your thoughts can easily pull you into a negativity trap. You will be given tools to prevent this from happening. In Week Five, you will learn one of the major misconceptions about emotions, the cost of suppressing your emotions, and tools to regulate difficult emotions. The following two Weeks, Six and Seven, focus on exercises designed to help you cultivate positive emotions and experience more joy in your life, which is something often overlooked and under taught. The final chapter, Week Eight, will help you to integrate everything you have learned. The order of the chapters here is intentional, in that it can be easier to grow positive emotional experiences after developing skills to dial down the intensity of negative thinking and challenging emotions. Throughout this book there is a common message that our bodily sensations, thoughts, emotions, and behaviors are intricately connected. By understanding and experiencing that connection, we can make changes in one area that will affect all three other areas.

This book is different than many other books in that it is not meant to be read in one or two sittings. Instead, I suggest that you read the first pages of Week One and then stop when you get to the first exercise. Set aside time to read this exercise and carry it out throughout the course of your day. All of these exercises are intended to take no more than 10 minutes, so that they can fit into even the busiest person's day.

The following day you can do the next exercise, and so on. If you find it helpful, you may also choose to repeat exercises before moving on, for as many days as you like. While this book provides eight weeks of guided, daily practices, it is important that you decide what pace would be most helpful for you to go through the exercises. Some people find it helpful to repeat particular exercises for several days before moving on to the next one; others find it helpful at the end of each chapter to practice integrating everything they have learned for several days or a week, before moving on. Some people may choose to focus on the exercises from one particular chapter, while others may want to sample several exercises from multiple chapters.

While the greatest benefit may come from experiencing all of the exercises in order over time, there can be benefits from approaching this material in any number of ways. There is no right or wrong way to do this, so find what works best for you. The important thing is to make the commitment to doing something, just ONE thing, every day. Sometimes that thing might be as small as just stopping and taking three deep breaths when you notice you are becoming stressed. It is important not to judge yourself by how much you accomplish in a given day or week, but simply to acknowledge each step you take.

Each chapter in this book follows a similar format. It begins with a goal/intention to highlight the skill in focus, and information on why this goal is important or relevant to your life. Following this are daily exercises designed to help wire in that particular skill. These exercises involve bringing relevant information into your field of awareness, noticing, imagining, taking actions, envisioning into the immediate future, calling up feelings and sensations in your body, writing, and using multiple modalities involving mind and body to help build new neural pathways. The accompanying worksheet for each day's practice is at the end of that week's chapter. This makes it easy to track what you have noticed each day and helps you follow through with each exercise.

Doing these worksheets, which take only a few minutes, is a critical part of this program. At the end of each chapter there is a visualization exercise to help integrate the material from that chapter. An audio of these visualization exercises, and some of the other exercises, can be found online at BethKurland.com, under the Books/Products tab so you may do them by listening to the recording, rather than trying to remember the text.

In addition, there is a writing exercise, a short affirmation that you can reflect on daily, and a summary of key take-away points at the end of each chapter, all intended to help you integrate the material from that week's chapter. The chapters are designed to be short and easy for the busy person to read, so that you can get right to work implementing the skills.

Like a diet book, you may change your way of eating and lose noticeable pounds in the first eight weeks. However, that is just the beginning. It is a lifestyle change that requires continued commitment, practice and action. This book is similar. If you follow the exercises in this book for eight weeks, I am certain you will experience positive changes in your life. But it is the continual daily commitment that will maintain your gains and help bring about long-term transformation. The more you do, the more momentum you will build, eventually making it easier and easier to maintain the gains you have made and implement the skills with less effort and thought.

I suggest that initially you go through this book in sequence, but it is designed in such a way that once you finish it, you can return to it again and again, picking and choosing your favorite exercises or the skills you most wish to work on, and making them a regular, daily part of your life.

As one Chinese proverb says: "To get through the hardest journey we need to take only one step at a time, but we need to keep on stepping." May this book help guide you and be your companion on your journey toward greater well-being.

HOW TO ACCESS THE AUDIOS ◀))) AND WORKSHEETS

In order to access and download the free daily worksheets that accompany this book, and to access the free guided audios that accompany certain of the exercises, visit BethKurland.com and click on the "Book/Products" tab.

The
TRANSFORMATIVE
POWER of
TEN MINUTES

WEEK ONE

THE COST OF STRESS & WHAT TO DO ABOUT IT

We Can't Change What We Don't See

"I had no idea how stressed out I was until I started paying attention! I realized how chronically tight my muscles were, how I have ongoing negative thoughts running through my head, a frequent feeling of unease, and irritability that tends to spill out to those around me. Having this awareness has become a cornerstone for change." —BARBARA

GOALS AND INTENTIONS FOR THIS WEEK

THIS WEEK, YOU WILL DISCOVER a new way to understand stress and learn about the cost of chronic stress in your life. You will learn that the physical sensations in your body, your thoughts, your emotions and your behaviors are intricately connected and why that is important. You will become skilled at noticing your own stress response, and you will learn how to interrupt this response and become more empowered and resilient in the face of stress. If this sounds helpful, read on! Like shining a flashlight in the darkness to reveal what is there, once we see our unhelpful, habitual ways of reacting to stress, we can choose a different response.

Why Is This Important?

One does not have to look far in books, medical journals, medical websites and the like to learn how chronic, daily stress has negative consequences for our health and well-being (American Psychological Association, 2012). It has been estimated that 75–90% of all medical illnesses are stress related (Robinson, 2013). Chronic stress has been associated with increased risk of heart disease, high blood pressure, diabetes, asthma, decreased immune functioning, headaches, gastrointestinal problems, obesity, accelerated aging, and premature death (National Institute of Mental Health). Besides the toll that stress can take on our bodies and minds, it has an emotional impact as well, such as contributing to increased anger, irritability, feelings of overwhelm, anxiety, and depression. These can have a negative impact on our relationships and on our sense of well-being and mental health. In addition, there are economic costs of stress, such as decreased productivity, missed days of work, and greater costs of health care due to stress related illness, which affect us on a global scale (Kalia, 2002). Clearly, having tools to manage and decrease the impact of stress can be beneficial in multiple ways.

What Is Stress?

When many people talk about stress, they describe it as something external to them (e.g., "my life is so stressful"). They may experience stress as a giant black cloud or a sense of being overwhelmed, without truly being aware of the specific triggers and ways that they contribute to or exacerbate their own experience of stress. Understanding stress in the context of the mind-body connection can be a powerful step towards making changes. In order to understand how best to cope with stress, it is helpful to think of stress as having four components: a physiological component (what is happening in our bodies); a cognitive component (our perceptions and thoughts about a particular situation); an emotional component (how we feel about a situation); and a subsequent behavioral component (how we act). When we realize that stress occurs on these four levels, and that each of these are not separate but instead are closely connected, we become more empowered to make changes in each of these areas. This week we will focus mostly on helping you observe and become more aware of your overall stress response, while in the forthcoming weeks we will address more specific ways to work with thoughts, emotions, and behaviors.

Let's look very briefly at what is happening in our bodies when we are stressed. As our brain perceives a threat, the hypothalamus (a structure in the middle of the brain that is a primitive part of our evolutionary inheritance from millions of years ago) becomes activated, turning on what is known as the fight-or-flight response. This response evolved to help us fight or flee from predators back in cave person days. Once a threat is perceived, the hypothalamus in turn stimulates the pituitary and adrenal glands, which set in motion a whole cascade of neurochemical reactions which release stress hormones, such as adrenaline and cortisol into our bloodstream, preparing our bodies to fight or flee (from a predator), or in some cases freeze (as in an animal playing dead). The modern day translation of this response might look more like arguing with someone because you believe you are right, fleeing by avoidance behaviors, such as procrastination, withdrawing, drinking, and numbing out, or freezing by becoming paralyzed with procrastination. Our modern day predators are no longer bears and other wild animals, but instead take the form of such things as financial pressures, having too much to do and not enough time, relationship conflicts, traffic jams, and work deadlines.

Our Evolutionary Inheritance

It turns out that this physiological reaction is an ancient part of our evolutionary inheritance, mediated by a branch of our autonomic nervous system called the sympathetic nervous system. Back in cave person days, it was quite adaptive to have a brain that could respond quickly to potential predators, alerting the body to either fight or flee. We survived as a species because of this response. For better or worse, that response is still with us in modern times. It can be useful when we are in rare but life threatening situations, such as jumping out of the way of an oncoming car, but it is much less useful for the modern threats we face on a daily basis such as traffic jams, arguments with coworkers or loved ones, demands of work and family, ongoing financial worries, and so on. As biologist Robert Sapolsky explains in his book *Why Zebras Don't Get Ulcers* (1994), back on the Savannah, when a zebra is chased by a lion, the fight-or-flight response is activated, and if the zebra is lucky, it will escape the lion's grasp. Once it is safe, the zebra's body returns very quickly to homeostasis, to the baseline relaxed state it was in before the lion appeared. Not so with modern day humans. When our fight-or-flight response is turned on, let's say by an argument with a loved one, or worries about finances, we can remain in a high arousal state by simply ruminating and stewing on the event in our minds, long after the initial argument or situation is over. Add to that all the other myriad of worries and stressors in a given day and it is easy to see how chronic stress can accumulate and be perpetuated by our own thinking (Cook, 2014).

In addition, when our fight-or-flight response is activated and our bodies are in survival mode, all of our internal resources are being mobilized to protect us from harm. Our blood is being shunted toward our fighting muscles, so the other functions of our bodies, such as digesting food, regenerating cells, and healing, are put on hold. Expending energy on our immune systems is not a priority when we are being chased by a lion. Back in ancient times, after the threat passed, the body would return to its normal resting state. However, you can see that if our bodies are in a chronic state of stress, as they often are in our modern culture, this can create health problems because our resources for digesting, regenerating, and healing are not fully available.

In addition to this evolutionary inheritance, we also inherited something from our ancestors referred to as a "negativity bias," which helps explain our human tendency to look for, see, and assume the worst (Hanson & Mendius, 2009). As neuroscientist Rick Hanson explains, our brain is like "Velcro for negative experiences and Teflon for positive ones" (Hanson & Mendius, 2009, p.68). As Hanson explains, back in ancient times this was adaptive because those who perceived a stick and immediately assumed it might be a snake were a lot more likely to survive than those who perceived a snake and thought that perhaps it was just a stick that could be ignored. So we have some odds stacked against us: We have a brain that is easily triggered by perceived threats, and we have a tendency to over-interpret situations as negative and threatening, and thus see the negatives more easily than the positives. Additionally, we live in a world where some stress is universal and inevitable. Because we are humans, we experience loss, illness, aging, death, and other inevitable parts of our human experience.

The Role of Our Perceptions

It is equally important to recognize that stress does not just happen TO us. It is how we perceive and interpret situations (the cognitive component mentioned above) that plays a big role in how we experience a situation, and how much we suffer because of it. Imagine, for example, Bob and Dean who are both laid off from the same job. Bob focuses on thoughts such as "I've been let go because I'm a failure; I can't do anything right; No one will want to hire me; I'm never going to find another job." Dean focuses on thoughts such as " I've been let go because economic times are difficult; hundreds of people were let go, not just me; I have good skills to offer someone; It may take awhile, but with enough persistence I know I can find something else." Who do you imagine will be more stressed? Following this example further, Bob will be more likely to feel emotionally upset, depressed, hopeless, (some emotional components of stress) while Dean will be more likely to feel hopeful and optimistic. In turn, Bob may tend to procrastinate, isolate, and turn to unhealthy ways of coping, such as drinking or overeating (behavioral aspects of stress), while Dean is more likely to actively look for another job, reach out to others for support, and take advantage of the extra time he has to take care of himself by exercising.

One of the goals of this chapter is to help you begin to have more choice over your stress response by becoming a more mindful observer of your experiences, both internal and external. I mentioned in the Introduction that mindfulness is a way of paying attention, in the present moment, without judging yourself. It is a way of observing what is happening inside of us and outside of us, simply noticing, without needing to react. The opposite of this is being in automatic pilot mode, going through the motions without awareness of the present moment. This latter mode is the common mode that most of us operate in. We are often caught up thinking about the past and future, instead of focusing on the here and now right in front of us. Think about a time when perhaps you drove somewhere, arrived at your destination, and had no recollection of the drive, what sights you passed, and what was unfolding before you each moment. When we go through life in this manner it is easy to experience life as "stressful" and it is easy to miss the small moments of beauty and meaning that, when woven together, can create greater joy and satisfaction.

*   *   *

On the following pages you will find a series of exercises which help you to recognize how stress shows up in your life; how you respond to stress in your body, thoughts, emotions, and behavior; how your thoughts contribute to the stress you experience; and what your common triggers are.

Imagine that you are in a pitch black room trying to get from point A to point B, but there are obstacles at nearly every step that you keep tripping on, making it difficult to move forward. Becoming a better observer of your experience is like being given a flashlight so that you can see in the dark where the obstacles are, and best decide a path that allows you to navigate around them. Let mindful awareness become your flashlight as it guides you through these exercises. (Note that we will focus more in depth on cultivating mindfulness skills in Week Three.)

> ## HOW TO ACCESS THE AUDIOS 🔊))) AND WORKSHEETS
>
> **The exercise worksheets for this book are located at the end of each chapter. Feel free to make copies as needed. You may also choose to access the free, guided audios that accompany certain of the exercises (indicated by the above audio symbol), and the free, downloadable, daily worksheets by visiting my website at BethKurland.com. Click on the "Book/Products" tab.**

EXERCISE ONE

Stress Thermometers

As you go through the day today, imagine that you have a thermometer that can measure your stress level on a scale of 1–10, where 1 is a very minimal level of stress and 10 is the highest level of stress that you might experience. Pause throughout the day, twice in the morning, twice in the afternoon, and twice at night (or more if you choose) and notice where your thermometer is at each time.

You might choose to set an alarm on your watch or phone to remind you to stop and take note at these various intervals throughout the day. Alternatively, I recommend using an app on your phone if possible such as Insight Timer® or Mindfulness Bell® (something that has pleasant sounds you can program to go off at set intervals of time) to remind you to stop and pay attention to this exercise, and the other ones in this book that follow.

In addition to these scheduled pauses, try to notice any times throughout the day when you feel stress creeping in.

When you pause, take a moment to record the number on your thermometer using the accompanying online worksheet, or your own notes. Stop and deliberately take a few breaths. If you are experiencing some level of stress, notice what is triggering you and write this down as well.

Take a few more deliberate breaths. This time notice what you are thinking to yourself right now, and write this down on the worksheet. Try to capture your thoughts on paper the way they sound in your head, just the way that you say them to yourself. It may take a little practice to capture them, as we often are not very aware of these automatic thoughts.

*   *   *

Tip: Recording your observations and experiences is a critical part of doing each of the exercises in the book. In addition to the worksheets at the end of the chapter, you can access free, downloadable worksheets on my website at BethKurland.com. Taking the time to write down your observations and insights, either in your own notebook, in the notes on your phone, or on the downloadable worksheets, will greatly increase the benefits of this book. Also, remember that you determine the pace of your journey.

You may choose to practice this exercise for several days, or move on after one day. At the end of this chapter you will have the opportunity to integrate all of the exercises from this chapter.

Example: When Barbara first tried this exercise her reminder alarm went off about an hour after she awoke. She was getting ready for work and getting her children ready for school. She noticed that she was a "6" on her stress scale. She became aware that she was triggered by the morning rush of trying to get a lot done at the house in the hour that she had to get everyone out the door. She noticed that she was thinking to herself "Oh god, I have a long day ahead of me. I have so much to do. It's gonna be a tough day."

Example: Maya became stressed and anxious as she began having a conversation with her husband about finances. She became aware after a few minutes into the conversation that she was having a stress response, and this awareness helped her become an observer of herself more closely. After the interchange, she noted that she was a "7" on her stress scale. It was triggered by discussion of money, and she had thoughts, such as "we'll never get out of this debt" and "this is awful."

EXERCISE TWO

Noticing Stress in Your Body

Today as you go through your day, see how many times you can catch yourself carrying tension in your body. Set a reminder alarm and take notice at least twice in the morning, twice in the afternoon, and twice at night of how your body is feeling.

Stop for a minute (at least a true 60 seconds, if not more) and take a few deep breaths. Scan your body from head to toe, noticing any places of tension or tightness in your body. As you consciously breathe, gently invite some breath into those areas that may feel tight or tense, imagining the muscles softening and releasing.

You can extend this practice by spending a few more minutes breathing in through your nose and out through your mouth. With each exhalation, choose an image such as an ice cube melting in hot water, knots unwinding or softening in the warm sun, or some other image that comes to mind, and invite your body and muscles to soften and loosen. Do not force this to happen—just allow what is there to be there, and if tension remains, simply notice it without judging it.

With each inhalation, you could imagine breathing in a feeling of peace and relaxation, a soothing color, or a feeling of warmth, or some other image that is comforting or relaxing to you. Allow yourself to welcome in these images, as well as the feeling of relaxation, while at the same time simply accepting where your body is at and not forcing anything. Simply notice what happens as you turn your awareness to your body and call up these various images in your mind.

Make sure to record your practice and observations on your worksheet.

Example: Mark was sitting at his desk at work when he remembered to check in and notice what was happening in his body. As he quickly scanned his body, he noticed that his shoulders were up by his ears and his chest was collapsed in, making it hard to take in a deep, full breath. As he took a few breaths, he gently let his shoulders drop down and he sat more upright. He imagined tension in his body being washed away and running down his body like rainwater, and as he breathed in, he imagined a soothing blue light travelling throughout his body. He did this for about 2 minutes at his desk. Afterwards, he was aware of feeling more calm and focused.

EXERCISE THREE

Adding Name Tags

As you go through your day today, and as you shine the light of awareness on your responses to stress, practice labeling your emotions by simply naming them (e.g., frustrated, angry, jealous, resentful, anxious, worried, etc.) When we take the time to differentiate what we are feeling (e.g., "I'm feeling panicky"; "I'm feeling irritable") rather than lumping all emotions into "I'm feeling stressed," or not naming them at all, we create a space in which to be with our feelings in a more compassionate way.

As with the previous exercises stop and notice any stress at least twice in the morning, twice in the afternoon, and twice at night. Make note of the intensity of your emotion on a 1–10 scale, and give the feeling a name. Importantly, if you are feeling minimal stress, stop and name what you *are* feeling just the same (e.g., "I feel peaceful"; "I feel content").

Once you identify the feeling, see if you can stay with it for a moment by simply bringing your awareness to that feeling. Notice how that feeling shows up in your body. Notice if the feeling shifts or changes as you hold your awareness on it. Some people fear that bringing awareness to their negative feelings will magnify or intensify them. Often, being mindful of our feelings does just the opposite. We will work more with this in Week Five, but this exercise will help lay an important foundation.

Record the information above and any accompanying observations on your worksheet.

Example: When Frank completed this exercise, he noticed he was getting stressed at his son for not cleaning his room. When he took a moment to shine the light of awareness on his stress and name it, he became aware first of a feeling of frustration. As he stayed with the feeling of frustration and noticed it in his body, he was surprised to discover that underneath the frustration was sadness. When he stayed with the sadness for a moment, he realized that he was feeling sad that his teenage son was growing up and pulling away from him.

Example: At work, Mark noticed his stress appeared when he became irritated at a coworker who didn't like his idea. As he became aware of and named the feeling of irritation, he also became aware of feelings of anger and inadequacy that he was holding onto from an earlier interchange with his brother, which he had not let go of.

EXERCISE FOUR

Past, Present and Future

Today you will practice noticing how often you are in the past, the future, or the present moment.

As often as you can remember, but at least a minimum of six times throughout the day, stop and ask yourself "is my mind focused on the past, the future, or what is happening right before me now?"

Places to stop and take note could include when you are taking a shower, eating a meal, talking to a colleague and/or loved one, driving, or any time you think of it. The idea is not to judge yourself if you catch yourself in the past or future, but simply to notice. Also notice if it was important that you were thinking about the past or future for a reason, or if your mind wandered there unnecessarily. There are times when reflecting on the past or planning for the future can be very useful (especially when doing so can bring about some kind of positive change or action), but notice how much of your past and future thinking tends to be ruminating about something that creates stress and cannot be changed. Notice how much of your stress is created by being caught up in thinking about trying to change something in the past or future that cannot be changed at all, or cannot be changed in that moment. Also, notice how much of the time your mind is "somewhere else" and you miss what is going on in front of you right here and now.

We will work more with our thinking in Weeks Three and Four, but for now just see what you notice using this exercise, and write down your observations.

Example: Winona was going for a walk around the lake in her town and began to observe her mind as she was walking. She was surprised to realize how little of the time she was in the present moment. She noticed herself thinking about everything she had to do later that day. She found herself thinking about an exchange that occurred recently with a coworker that upset her. She also found herself thinking about getting tense about her parents who were coming to visit this weekend, and noticed how she began imagining various possible things that could happen that would upset her when they arrived. She was able to laugh to herself when she noticed this, realizing that she was creating double stress for herself: stress thinking about it even before it happened, as well as the actual stress that the visit itself might bring. Each time she caught herself in these past or future thoughts, she realized that she was missing out on the beauty right in front of her. When she recorded her observations, she noted on her worksheet that for each time she was in the past or future, there was nothing she could do about it in that moment.

EXERCISE FIVE

Noticing Behaviors and Choices

Today you will notice how your experience of stress shows up in your behaviors and choices throughout the day. You will also become more aware of where you do and don't have choice regarding your stress response. For example, you may not have a choice about your initial physical and emotional reaction to upsetting news or a troubling situation, but you do have a choice over how you respond to that situation as it unfolds.

Pick three times today when you notice your stress thermometer rising from its baseline. Your task is to observe yourself and notice your behavior choices:

How are you reacting to the situation?

What are you doing—or not doing?

What are you saying?

How are you acting if you are around others?

If someone else were watching you, what would they see you doing?

Write this down on your worksheet. Then, write down whether or not you had control over this behavior, and write down an alternative behavioral response in the last column.

> *Example:* Richard was at work and discovered that one of the people who he manages sent out an email with incorrect information, which could have potential negative repercussions for the company. Furious, he stormed over to this person and started reprimanding him. A short while later, when he recorded his behavior, he realized that he could not control his initial upset, but could have chosen perhaps a more effective way to talk with his employee and handle his own stress.

> *Example:* Miranda got off the phone with her ex-husband, who was completely unsupportive of a situation regarding their son, and unwilling to use consistent parenting strategies to address the situation. She was angry and hurt. She caught herself a few minutes later eating a bag of junk food mindlessly, even when she was not hungry. While she realized she may not have been able to control her initial emotional response of upset, she became aware that her unhealthy eating was certainly within her control, and that there were more helpful behaviors, such as calling a friend or writing in her journal or going for a walk, that she could do when upset.

EXERCISE SIX

Calling Up a Current Stressor (Putting Together What You Have Learned)

Set aside at least five or 10 minutes for this exercise, preferably first thing in the morning or even before you get out of bed. (If you like, you can access a free audio of this exercise at BethKurland.com, under the Books/Products tab.) Call up a stressful recent past event in your mind, ideally something in the last week or few days that is fresh in your memory.

Allow yourself for a moment to reexperience this event in your mind. As you do, notice what is happening in your body. See if you can feel the stress that you felt, and observe where it shows up in your body. Notice, for example, whether it is a tightness, a clenching, a hardening, a closing off, or some other sensation.

When you have a sense of what is happening in your body, take a moment to notice what is happening in your mind:

What stress thoughts are you having?

How accurate are these thoughts? Are they irrational, extreme, or forecasting into the future? Do they call up past events of other times you might have felt like this? See if you can pause and name the feelings that you are experiencing.

Notice if there are many feelings, or one primary feeling.

Notice the intensity of the feeling.

Finally, notice how you chose to act and behave in this situation. Did you raise your voice; shut down or get quiet; say or do something you later felt bad about; take an action that was productive or unproductive in some way?

When you have a complete sense of the four dimensions of this experience, (your physical sensations, emotions, thoughts and behaviors) take a minute to write down your observations on your worksheet.

As you go through your day today, pay close attention to these four dimensions of stress. Catch yourself one time today when you begin to feel stress and notice each of these four dimensions of stress as you did in the imagery exercise above. Record these on your worksheet.

Example: Karen had planned a week ahead and rearranged her schedule to have the plumber come this particular day. When she received a phone call from the plumber saying that he was unable to come because something came up, she could feel immediately an increased tension in her body. This tension was most prominent in her neck and shoulders. She felt irritable, angry and disappointed. She began to have stressful thoughts such as "How am I going to fit this in next week?" and "This just ruined my whole day." She observed that she started to get snappy at her children for things that she might not react to if she were relaxed. Normally, she would have started to yell at her children and perhaps even mistakenly blame them for her bad mood and stress; however, because she was observing her own behavior, she caught and stopped herself from going down this path.

EXERCISE SEVEN

Visualization for Stress Reduction

Note: This, and some similar exercises later in the book, are inspired by psychologist Daniel Brown, Ph.D., director of the Center for Integrative Psychotherapy in Newton, Massachusetts. Dr. Brown is an internationally renowned speaker, teacher, and author in the areas of trauma, hypnosis, and meditation. I had the privilege of taking several workshops with him over the years and use a modification of what he called the "TV technique" often with my patients. This exercise is in part inspired by that technique.

This exercise will require you to set aside about 10 minutes. You are encouraged to listen to the accompanying online audio (available at BethKurland.com under the tab "Books/Products") to guide you through this exercise, although you may also follow the instructions here and do it on your own if you prefer.

Take a moment and find a comfortable seated position. Begin to bring your awareness into your body as you notice the sensation of your feet connected to the ground beneath you. Feel the soles of your feet and the pressure of your feet on the earth beneath you.

Notice all of the places that your body makes contact with the surface upon which you are sitting. Experience an upright feeling in your spine as you are aware at the same time of the pull of gravity that keeps you seated.

Take a moment now and turn your awareness to your breathing. Follow your breathing as you inhale, and as you exhale. Continue to follow your breath as it comes in and out.

When you feel ready, imagine that you are watching a movie of a typical day in your life. At first as you watch this movie, you will see some of your habitual responses to the stress in your life that have not been so helpful to you. As you watch yourself go through a typical day, begin to notice how stress shows up and what its most common triggers are for you. As you shine the light of awareness on this scene, you begin to notice very clearly how stress manifests in your body, and all the ways that your body holds tension.

You might see yourself unconsciously tightening your muscles throughout the day, or assuming a posture that reflects the stress, or perhaps having body language or facial gestures which reveal the stress you are feeling.

Take a moment to name some of the challenging emotions you typically experience in your day and week. Do you tend to feel overwhelmed, frustrated, anxious, worried, angry, irritable, etc.?

As you see your day and week unfolding before you on the screen, notice what you are thinking to yourself when you get stressed.

Are those thoughts helpful or unhelpful?

Are they judgmental, compassionate, self-demeaning, rational or irrational?

What are you doing in these scenes when faced with challenging emotions?

Become aware of all of the ways that you behave and react that may not be most beneficial to you and your well-being. Take as much time as you need to truly get a sense of how this feels for you as you watch yourself, and how this feels for you when you handle stress in this manner.

How does it affect your week? How does it affect those around you?

When you are ready, I invite you to replay these scenes again, but this time as you watch yourself, you are able to see yourself going through the day with more ease and less stress. You are able to see ways in which you notice the tension in your body but choose to release it. You are able to notice how you name your emotions, and bring awareness to what you are feeling.

As you do this, you can watch as this helps you to have more insight into what you are experiencing. You may even notice that some of these feelings are not attached to this particular situation, but are feelings triggered by something that happened in the past.

You notice that naming your emotions helps to demystify what you are experiencing, and may even lessen the intensity of the moment just slightly. As you observe yourself going through your day and week, notice how catching your stress thoughts helps to keep you from getting so pulled into them.

You may even see yourself saying more helpful, realistic thoughts to yourself such as "this is hard, but I'll get through this," "though this is uncomfortable, it isn't the end of the world," or catching yourself from focusing on something in the past or future and pulling yourself back to the present moment and to what is happening right here and now.

As you see yourself facing THIS moment, you realize that right now, in this moment, you can handle what is happening. See yourself making the kind of choices that will help you feel better, and bring greater ease and well-being into your life. Instead of being reactive, you might see yourself being more thoughtful and handling situations in a proactive, productive manner, or perhaps accepting the challenge you are facing with more compassion.

As you watch the completion of this "movie" for right now, notice how it feels in your body to handle stress in healthy ways, and to experience greater ease in your day and week. Allow this feeling to become familiar to you, notice where it "lives" in you; hold onto a felt sense of it. Let this feeling grow inside of you so that it begins to fill you up. Let this feeling of ease and confidence in handling stress in your life become solid within you.

As you focus on this feeling right now, pick something to help remind you of this feeling. It could be a physical sensation in your body right now, like an open feeling in your heart or the feeling of your shoulders being completely relaxed. It could be a thought or phrase or word such as "relax" or "I can choose my reactions." It may be an image or symbol or color. Whatever comes to mind right now—let that become your link to help you remember and call up this feeling whenever you choose.

Now, whenever you are ready, take a few deep, slow breaths, and bring your awareness back into the room.

WRITING ACTIVITY

DEVELOPING YOUR DE-STRESS ACTION PLAN

Take some time to review all the worksheets you filled out from this chapter. Reflect on all your observations and what you have learned so far about yourself. Take time to notice how stress tends to show up in your life and how you responded to it in each of the four dimensions that we have explored: physically, emotionally, cognitively and behaviorally.

How does increased awareness of your stress response create more choices for you in how you handle stress?

Are there things that you can do proactively to decrease stress in your life?

Working within each of the four dimensions, come up with ways that you could make small changes that might help build resources to cope with future stressors. See the examples below for some ideas, and then come up with some for yourself. Use the Developing Your De-Stress Action Plan worksheet on page 29 to create an action plan for how you can decrease your response to stress in your life.

Example: Barbara noticed that one of her major stress triggers was feeling rushed in the morning trying to get everyone out of the house. In order to help with this, she decided to make a few small proactive changes which included setting her alarm for 10 minutes earlier, making the lunches the night before, and putting her children in charge of picking out their clothes and packing their backpacks the night before. Another thing that Barbara became aware of from doing these exercises was that she had a tendency to project into the future about how tough her day was going to be before it even got started. She decided to replace these stress thoughts with more realistic and helpful thoughts such as "I'm feeling rushed in this moment but this does not predict the rest of my day."

Example: When Mark became aware of how much tension he was holding in his body at his desk each day, he decided to schedule several short breaks throughout the day where he simply gets up and walks around for 2 minutes. During these 2 minutes, he chooses to consciously focus on taking some slow deep breaths, and dropping and relaxing his shoulders.

Example: Frank found it helpful to name and notice the emotions that were behind his feelings of "stress." He realized that often he tends to take his stress out on the kids and others around him when there may be other underlying feelings that he is responding to from past situations. Based on what he learned about himself, he decided that before he reprimands his children, he will take a moment to stop and name what he is feeling. He will pay particular attention to how much that feeling is tied to something happening in the present moment versus something that happened in the past.

Example: Miranda became aware of how often she tended to turn to mindless eating as a way to numb out her feelings of stress or upset. This increased awareness opened up an opportunity to make a different choice when she found herself feeling upset.

WEEKLY REFLECTION

Note: You can find a copy of this and other weekly reflections on the downloadable handouts. You may wish to print it out and hang it in a visible place, such as your bathroom mirror or fridge, to remind yourself of what you are working on.

- This week I choose to notice stress in my body.
- I choose to notice stressful thoughts when they arise.
- I choose to observe my habitual way of reacting to stress.
- While I recognize stress is inevitable, I am willing to also recognize the part I play in reacting to stress in unhealthy ways, and in ways that may exacerbate or even create the stress I experience.

- As I shine the light of awareness on my experience, (my thoughts, feelings, sensations and behaviors) I allow myself to step out of automatic pilot and embrace the present moment.

- The present moment is really the only moment in which I can ever truly live.

KEY SUMMARY POINTS

- We have an evolutionary predilection toward an easily activated stress response (the fight-or-flight response) triggered by *perceived* threats as well as real ones, in combination with our inherited "negativity bias."

- While stress is an inevitable part of life, there are many aspects of stress over which we can learn to have choice and control.

- Stress is not something that simply happens to us. It is a complex series of physiological, emotional, cognitive, and behavioral components which act together to make up our experience of "stress." Our interpretations and perceptions of situations play a large role in how much stress we experience.

- By increasing our awareness of our stress response, we increase the choices that we have to react to stressors in our lives.

- Our thinking tends to be focused in the past or future, which can increase our experience of stress, and take us away from feelings of well-being and joy in this moment. By learning to become more aware of when our minds are in the past, present and future, we can cultivate a greater connection with the present moments in our lives.

Week 1, Exercise 1 **STRESS THERMOMETERS**		
	Stress Thermometer (1–10)	**Situation/Trigger**	**Accompanying Thoughts**
Morning			
Afternoon			
Evening			

©2017 Beth Kurland, Ph.D.

Week 1, Exercise 2 **NOTICING STRESS IN YOUR BODY**			
	Stress Thermometer (1–10)	Situation/Trigger	Physical Sensations	Observations
Morning				
Afternoon				
Evening				

©2017 Beth Kurland, Ph.D.

Week 1, Exercise 3 **ADDING NAME TAGS**			
	Situation/Trigger	Emotions	Intensity (1–10)	Observations
Morning				
Afternoon				
Evening				

©2017 Beth Kurland, Ph.D.

Week 1, Exercise 4 **PAST, PRESENT AND FUTURE**		
	Situation	Are thoughts in past, present or future	Observations
Morning			
Afternoon			
Evening			©2017 Beth Kurland, Ph.D.

	Week 1, Exercise 5 **NOTICING BEHAVIORS AND CHOICES**		
	Situation/Trigger	Reaction (What am I doing/saying) Control over Behavior (yes/no)	Alternative Behavioral Response
Morning			
Afternoon			
Evening			

©2017 Beth Kurland, Ph.D.

Week 1, Exercise 6	
🔊)))	**CALLING UP A CURRENT STRESSOR** **(Putting Together What You Have Learned)**

Current Stressful Situation	
Stress Thermometer (1–10)	
Physical Sensations	
Emotions	
Thoughts	
Behaviors	

©2017 Beth Kurland, Ph.D.

Week 1, Exercise 7

🔊)) **VISUALIZATION FOR STRESS REDUCTION**

Observations from watching the first "movie":

Note physical sensations:	Emotions
	Thoughts
	Behaviors
In what way are your thoughts helpful or unhelpful?	
In what way are your reactions helpful or unhelpful?	
How does your reaction affect your day/week?	
How does your reaction affect those around you?	

Observations from watching the second "movie":

Note physical sensations	Emotions
	Thoughts
	Behaviors
In what way are your thoughts helpful or unhelpful?	
In what way are your reactions helpful or unhelpful?	
How does your reaction affect your day/week?	
How does your reaction affect those around you?	

Week 1, Writing Activity
DEVELOPING YOUR DE-STRESS ACTION PLAN

Write out your de-stress action plan here:

Week Two

DEVELOPING A ROADMAP

It's Easier to Change Your Behavior If You Know Where You Are Headed & Why You Are Going There In the First Place

*"I had never stopped and taken the time to really identify what was most important to me in different areas of my life. Doing so has helped me see where I most need to make changes in order to be my best self. I am now motivated to start making those changes, and already I have experienced more balance in my life." —*LEROY

LAST WEEK, YOU LEARNED THAT YOUR THOUGHTS, feelings, physical sensations, and behaviors are all intricately connected, and that stress can affect all of these areas. You developed some insight into how stress shows up in your life. This understanding creates the foundation for making important changes (we will work on this further in the coming weeks). However, before we get there, we need to have a roadmap and some motivation for change.

GOALS AND INTENTIONS FOR THIS WEEK

This week, you will discover what matters most to you in different areas of your life and see how this knowledge can create motivation to choose actions that are in line with your values. You will learn to recognize some of the obstacles that get in the way of having the life you want, and you will develop a willingness to experience some emotional discomfort along the way if it means living a more meaningful life.

Why Is This Important?

In order to make lasting changes in our behavior, we have to want to do so. We need to be motivated to change old habits and put in the effort to bring about new results. Remember, it can be easier to follow that well-worn path in the woods than to forge a new pathway, because the latter takes more conscious effort.

Most people are comfortable staying with old routines and habitual ways of operating in the world, even if that is not necessarily the most satisfying or beneficial for them. To overcome this inertia, it can be helpful to remind ourselves of the reasons why we are putting in effort to change, and holding this knowledge out like a beacon of light to guide us towards a new way of being. For example, imagine someone who is overweight and wants to lose weight. If they identify that one of the qualities they most value is to be healthy and energetic so they can run around and be active with their children and not miss out on these experiences, holding on to this as a value can guide and motivate them to overcome unhealthy urges in a way that simply focusing on the goal of reducing numbers on a scale may not. Likewise, if a person identifies that one of the qualities that is most important to them as an employee is being a contributing member of their company, then they may be more motivated to push through their social anxiety in order to share their ideas and speak up, because they realize that doing so will bring more meaning into their work life.

The ideas in this chapter are inspired from Acceptance and Commitment Therapy (ACT), which is an empirically based psychological intervention developed by Steven Hayes (Hayes, Strosahl & Wilson, 1999). One aspect of ACT is to help people identify their personal values in order to encourage them to take committed actions to bring more meaning into their lives. These values, defined for the purpose of this book as the qualities that are most important to us, can serve as a kind of roadmap for us on the journey through this book and through life.

In addition, identifying what is most important to us can help us to make behavior choices in line with our life goals despite strong emotions that might otherwise stop us (e.g., pain, anxiety, depression, stress). One of the core concepts of ACT is that much psychological suffering is caused by something called "experiential avoidance" (Luoma, Hayes & Walser, 2007). In simple terms, when we run up against uncomfortable emotions (such as stress, sadness, anxiety, pain, etc.) we often do everything we can to avoid feeling these uncomfortable feelings, even if this means that we stop ourselves from engaging in meaningful and valued aspects of our lives. As an example, think about a person who stops going to public places they used to enjoy because doing so brings about some anxiety; or a person who avoids intimate relationships for fear that they might experience loss. ACT teaches us that we don't have to get rid of our unwanted emotions in order to live the lives we want. Instead, we can learn to accept whatever we are feeling (not push it away) and take the emotional discomfort along for the ride while we pursue what is most important and meaningful to us.

We will work more in depth with accepting our emotions in Week Five, but will begin to explore it in the exercises that follow. You will have the opportunity here to identify the qualities that are most important to you and to work on choosing behaviors and changing behaviors that align with the most important qualities of who you want to be. These exercises are inspired by the work of Steven Hayes (2005) and the Bull's Eye exercise developed by Swedish ACT therapist Tobias Lundren, as referenced by Russ Harris (2013). I often use this exercise with my patients and have adapted it here for you through an experiential meditation.

Identifying What Qualities Are Most Important in Your Day's "Work"

For the purpose of this exercise, "work" can be whatever you spend a majority of your time doing, whether it is working in an office, taking care of children at home, creating artwork, volunteering, or taking care of the house and finances. Set aside a minimum of 5 minutes to go through the initial part of this exercise. It is best done first thing in the morning, and could even be done before you get out of bed. Alternatively, you could do this at night, and then proceed to part two the next day. Ideally, set aside some quiet, uninterrupted time to do this exercise. You may use the recorded audio for this exercise (access online) if you like, or you may choose to do it on your own.

Take a moment to reflect on what you most value about your current life's work.

What qualities do you wish to bring to your work, and which ones are most important to you? This is not about identifying specific goals (such as wanting to get a raise, sell a product or work at a particular company), but rather about discovering the underlying qualities that you would like to bring to your work to make it more meaningful and help increase your sense of well-being in your workplace.

Some qualities that you might value most could include:
- having confidence in what you do;
- being compassionate or friendly;
- feeling a sense of balance and ease as you go through your day;
- being reliable and dependable;
- bringing creative ideas to others.

As you bring these qualities into your awareness, imagine what it would look like and feel like to have those qualities show up in your work day today. If you have a hard time imagining this, you might think about someone you respect who embodies and lives these values, and imagine what it looks like as they go through their day. Then imagine yourself in their shoes.

How would you act in ways that would convey what is most important to you? How would you speak to others? See yourself acting in those ways.

What does your posture and body language look like when you do this? If confidence is important to you, how would you stand and carry yourself? If compassion or friendliness is important, how might your body reflect a position of openness, connection or willingness to listen or engage with others?

How does it FEEL in your body to be bringing these qualities into your work?

Invite this feeling into your body right now and let it linger there. If you were embodying this quality today, what would you be thinking and saying to yourself? Tell yourself these thoughts right now. Take as much time as you need to call up in as much detail as possible what it would look and feel like to create a sense of well-being in the workplace through your own thoughts and actions.

When you have a good sense of this, take a few minutes and write down what you noticed during this exercise. On the worksheet, identify what qualities about yourself are most important to you at work and any accompanying body sensations, feelings, thoughts, and behaviors that go along with these qualities.

Part Two: As you go through your day today, notice how aligned your actions are with what you identified as being most important to you. Note how close or far off the mark you are from living the life you want at work. Make note of this on the worksheet.

Don't judge yourself, but simply see this exercise as an opportunity to give yourself helpful information. Also, notice what prevents you from attaining these qualities in your life and having the experience you want at work. What are your roadblocks?

Are there any difficult emotions that you might be avoiding feeling that play a role in keeping you from taking actions to experience optimal wellness at your work?

Write these roadblocks down on your worksheet.

> *Example:* Leroy identified that one of the qualities he most values for himself is having balance at work so that he is not overly stressed and overworked, and is productive instead of drained. He could imagine this easily as he envisioned himself looking relaxed, smiling, joking with coworkers, and leaving work at 5 p.m. In the initial exercise, he noticed his muscles relaxed, and he experienced an open and energetic feeling in his body. He thought, "I enjoy my job. I have a lot to offer." As he went through his actual day, he recognized that he was fairly far off the mark from having this experience of balance at work. The roadblock that most gets in his way, he realized, is his inability to say "no" to extra demands placed on him. The feeling he is avoiding is one of disappointing others and letting others down, and the discomfort that this causes him, even when taking on this extra work is technically voluntary and clearly burdensome to him.

EXERCISE TWO

Identifying What Qualities Are Most Important in Your Family Relationships

For the purpose of this exercise, "family" can refer to partners, spouses, children, parents, siblings, extended family, or anyone you consider as family. Note that you will have an opportunity to explore relationships that involve non-family members in another exercise.

As you did in the previous exercise, set aside a minimum of 5 minutes to go through the initial part of this exercise. Feel free to use the audio to guide you with this if you wish. You will be following the instructions from the first exercise, but instead of focusing on the workplace you will take a moment to reflect on what qualities you would most like to bring to your family relationships. Again, this is not about specific goals, such as "I want to call my parents three times a week" or "I want to propose to my fiancé by June."

Instead, ask yourself: Who do I want to be, what kind of person do I most want to be, when it comes to being a part of my family. Perhaps one quality about yourself that is most important is being a good listener for your partner; being present with your children on a regular basis; being supportive and loving to your parents, or being able to set better boundaries with family members.

Ask yourself what qualities will bring about the greatest sense of well-being for you in your family. Now, follow the instructions from above and imagine how you would feel going through your day living as this person.

When you get to the end of this exercise, be sure to use the worksheet to identify what qualities about yourself are most important to you in your family, and any accompanying physical body sensations, feelings, thoughts, and behaviors that go along with these qualities

Part Two: Follow the instructions as in the exercise above, but this time as you go through your day, notice how aligned your actions are with what you identified as being most important to you in your family.

Fill out the accompanying worksheet, and make note of any roadblocks that get in your way of being the person you most want to be in your family.

Are you avoiding experiencing any difficult emotions that might prevent you from taking actions that would help you achieve a feeling of optimal wellness in your family relationships?

Examples: Jessica noted that one of the qualities most important to her in her family was to be more present with her children. She was able to call up a sense of this easily by thinking about times when she *was* very present with her children. She was able to stay with this experience, notice it and put her attention on it so that it felt very real and clear to her. She felt happy, relaxed, spontaneous, and attentive. She visualized herself playing on the floor with her children and laughing. She imagined thinking to herself "this time with my children is valuable. I don't want to look back and regret missing this." She realized as she went through her day that she was somewhat off the mark from where she wanted to be. Her main roadblock was a feeling of needing to achieve, accomplish and not "sit around"— something that she knew came from her own family of origin. She recognized that when she was not "accomplishing something" she felt anxious, and so she avoided this anxious feeling by constantly doing, even if this meant that she often missed playful, spontaneous moments with her children.

For Luda, the quality that was most important to her was being able to set firm limits with her family and not feel taken advantage of by them. She was able to call up a clear image of exhibiting this quality by thinking of a close friend who is very good at setting limits and boundaries. She imagined the kinds of things that her friend might do and say in order to help her embody this experience for herself. What she realized from going through this exercise is that she is far from where she wants to be in this area, and that she caters to certain family members' needs to avoid feeling the discomfort of their distress and disapproval, even if it means putting her own needs aside entirely.

EXERCISE THREE

Identifying What Is Most Important for Your Personal Health and Self-Care

This exercise follows the same format as the previous exercises. You may follow along with the guided audio if you like. To begin, take some time to reflect on what is most important to you in the area of your life involving your health (this could be physical, emotional, spiritual, and/or mental) and the ways that you care for yourself.

As you reflect on optimal wellness in this area of your life, what qualities would you like to experience that would contribute to your well-being? For example, for some people, feeling healthy and energetic might be of prime importance to them; others might value feeling calm and centered as they go through their day; for others, feeling focused, organized and productive might be qualities that help them feel their best; for still others, feeling a spiritual connection within themselves and in their lives allows them to best take care of themselves. Proceed from here as instructed in the previous exercise, incorporating both parts one and two into this exercise.

Examples: Justin was keenly aware that one of the qualities most important to him in this area of his life involves being organized and focused. He was able to call up a feeling of this quality by thinking about a time in his life when he felt most organized and focused, when he was in graduate school. He recalled feeling a sense of clarity, calmness, and pride, which he felt in his body during this exercise, as he thought about this previous time in his life and as he imagined what his life would look like today with those same qualities present. He imagined saying to himself "my life flows more easily when things are organized. This feels good." He realized that he is not currently experiencing this quality in his life to the extent that he wants because he is avoiding the anxiety that his disorganization causes him when he tries to face it. As he went through his day, he noticed how easy it was for him to procrastinate and engage in other avoidance behaviors.

Carol found from doing this exercise that the quality that is most important to her is one of self-care regarding her physical health. She realized that she falls short of bringing this quality into her own life because she has difficulty setting aside time in her busy day to take care of herself. When she tried this exercise, it felt somewhat "foreign" to her to visualize taking time out to care for herself in such ways as going for a walk, preparing healthy meals, or going to a yoga class, though these things felt good to her when she could imagine them. She could best get a sense of what this might feel like by imagining her boss, who she considers a good role model, doing these activities, and then envisioning these feelings within herself. She thought, "I am worth taking care of." Carol noted that she is very far from living these values, and her biggest obstacles are her feelings of guilt for taking time to herself, and fears of others judging and evaluating her if she goes to a yoga class. She noticed how she avoids this guilt and fear by not taking action.

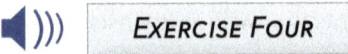

EXERCISE FOUR

Identifying What Qualities Are Most Important in Your Non-Family Relationships

For this exercise, you will identify the qualities you most value in yourself in relationships outside of your family. This could involve friends, coworkers, neighbors, or the community at large. As we have done with the other exercises, take a moment to reflect on what is most important to you in outside relationships in your life.

Qualities that might be most important to you could include:
- wanting to be a loyal and devoted friend to others;
- experiencing a sense of involvement and connection with your community;
- being friendly and helpful to those around you;
- treating the people you manage with dignity and respect.

Take some time to follow the instructions from Exercise One above to complete this exercise. You may follow along with the audio if you wish.

Examples: When Russell went through this exercise he identified that treating his employees with respect was an important quality that he valued in himself. He could clearly envision going through his day and bringing this quality into his interactions, because much of the time he is able to do this in his life. He was able to get a strong sense of how this feels within him when he does this, and noted that it gave him a feeling of well-being and pride. What he noticed, however, is that when he perceives someone is taking advantage of him, or thwarting his progress toward success, he can all too quickly lose sight of what is most important to him and react in anger; he does not think before he speaks. When he does this, he regrets his actions shortly afterwards. While he was not aware of avoiding a particular feeling in this case, he noted that a major obstacle for him was the tendency to be swept away very quickly by intense emotions.

Lynne was able to quickly identify that an important quality for her in relationships was being herself and feeling connected through time spent together. This is not something she has experienced recently since her move to a new state, as she is painfully shy and avoids interacting with people for fear they will judge her and not like her. In order to imagine what being truly authentic and feeling connected to others might feel like, she had to recall the time before she moved and remember what this used to feel like. When she did this, she was able to access a positive feeling of connection and openness within herself. She envisioned having such thoughts as "I'm a kind, caring and fun person to be around when I let people get to know me."

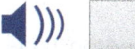 **EXERCISE FIVE**

Identifying What Qualities Are Most Important in Your Personal Time

In this exercise, the final domain we will explore is the area of personal time.

Take a moment to think about what qualities are most important for you to cultivate when it comes to your personal time. Do you most want your personal time to be:

- an opportunity to experience a sense of replenishment and renewal;
- the chance to be creative and express yourself in the world;
- a time to experience feeling passionate and alive by doing what you love;
- a way to experience solitude through connection with the natural world; or,
- perhaps an opportunity to experience service to others.

Whatever is most important to you, call that up and follow the format laid out in the Exercise Five worksheet on page 50. Feel free to follow along with the audio if that is helpful.

> *Example:* Sapir identified that an important quality he wanted to cultivate through his personal time was the ability to feel restored by connecting with nature. He was very easily able to call up what this feels like by recalling times when he used to hike in the local state park, or fish in the lake. When he envisioned doing these things, he immediately had a peaceful, serene feeling in his body. He had thoughts to himself about how grateful he was to be alive and enjoy this time. While his life used to be very aligned with this value, he has found his time stretched thin since having children, and he has let go of this part of his life. He did not experience avoidance of any particular emotions in this case, but was aware of not prioritizing this in his life.

EXERCISE SIX

Putting Things in Perspective to Work through Roadblocks

Today we will look more closely at the roadblocks and obstacles that you have identified in the previous exercises, in each of the five areas of your life. You will need to refer to your previous worksheets from this chapter to complete this exercise.

First, make a list of each of the roadblocks that you identified. (You can use the worksheet that accompanies this exercise to do so.)

Next, identify one roadblock on your list and use the following questions to help you step back and take some perspective on this issue:

1. Ask yourself "if I were to work through this obstacle and face it head on, what might I do differently?

2. Will there be any significant negative consequences in a week, or a month, or a year from now?

3. Am I willing to work through this roadblock, even if it means feeling some discomfort, in order to live a more meaningful life? What might I gain by doing so?

Write down the answers to these questions for each roadblock.

Examples: Leroy realized that saying "no" at work to voluntary requests might feel uncomfortable in the moment, but would not matter in the grand scheme of things, because he is a hard and conscientious worker and does not need to do it all and please everyone all the time. Feeling uncomfortable about disappointing others on occasion by saying "no" might be worth it if he could feel less stressed, more productive at work overall, and experience more balance in his life.

Jessica found the question—will this matter in a year—quite helpful and even amusing. She realized that turning off her cellphone and leaving dirty dishes in the sink for a short while to play with her children, would certainly not matter in a week or month from now. She thought that she would be willing to sit with the anxiety of a messy house for a short period of time if it meant she could have more quality time with her children.

Carol was able to use this perspective taking exercise to recognize that taking an hour to herself several times a week would not greatly impact other family member's needs in the course of a month or year, but it would go a long way to helping her stay healthy. She might be willing to experience some embarrassment—showing up for a yoga class if it meant that she could feel more well-being in her life.

Russell recognized through this exercise that the day to day things that anger him at work probably won't be relevant a year from now, but how he sees himself as an employer will be. While he is not sure how to keep his anger from getting the best of him (this will be addressed more in subsequent weeks), he is willing to be more aware of his emotions and how he reacts to them.

While Luda was not sure what negative consequences might arise if she were to set firm boundaries with outside family members (might they not talk to her for a period of time? might they not invite her to a gathering?) she doubted that these would be lasting or affect her long term relationship with them. She also recognized that taking care of her own needs was worth it, even if it meant someone might be disapproving or upset with her.

Sapir found that if he were to carve out a small amount of time each week for himself, there would be no lasting or long term negative consequences. It might mean needing to give up something else for that time, but if doing so would be restorative to him it might be worth it.

Visualization – Putting It All Together

You will need to set aside about 10 minutes for this exercise. It may work best if you can follow along with the audio, but if not you can use the text below to guide you.

For this visualization exercise, you will imagine that you are living your life in perfect alignment with the qualities that you identified in the previous exercises. (You will notice some similarity in places here with the earlier exercises. This is intentional and is meant to help create a clearer blueprint for you, and an opportunity to wire these qualities in more strongly.)

Begin by getting into a comfortable position where you can remain for about 10 minutes. Take a moment to feel the bottoms of your feet connected with the ground beneath you.

As you breathe in, imagine drawing up breath from the bottom of your feet all the way to the top of your head. As you breathe out, allow the exhalation to travel all the way down your body and into your feet.

Take the next minute to focus on your inhalation and your exhalation, gently bringing your attention back to your breath if it wanders away.

Now, think about the quality that is most important to you in your day's "work." As you imagine yourself going through the coming week, see yourself living your life by embracing this quality, and taking actions that fully bring this quality into your life.

Clearly see yourself taking those actions as you focus on what is most important to you at work. As you watch this scene unfold, you will have a clear vision of what roadblocks and obstacles get in your way of living this value. As those obstacles arise in your week, see yourself coming up with creative and helpful solutions to work around and through those obstacles.

If there are any emotions that you are avoiding, and if that avoidance stops you from living a meaningful life in this area, picture yourself as willing to tolerate some temporary discomfort in your emotional experience to have the life that you want. As you see yourself living a meaningful life through your work, take some time to notice how this feels in your body.

Identify what sensations are present, where in your body you feel them, and what these sensations feel like. Let this feeling become familiar by focusing on the feeling and taking a snapshot of it in your mind so that you can remember it and call it up later.

Take some time to notice what you are thinking to yourself when you are living your life from this quality that is so important to you.

When this experience feels complete, go on to explore and envision your life being in alignment with the qualities that are most important to you in your family relationships. Follow the same format as above, and then proceed to envision embodying the qualities you most want in non-family relationships, with personal health and self-care, and with your personal time.

Make sure to see yourself working through any obstacles that arise in your pursuit of these values.

WRITING ACTIVITY

DEVELOPING AN ACTION PLAN

Set aside at least 10 minutes for this activity. Take some time to look over all of your worksheets and identify what qualities are most important to you, and which ones feel furthest away from how you are currently living your life.

Choosing those, or working with all five areas, write out some small, concrete action steps that you can take starting right now, to help you move closer to living that valued aspect of your life. Notice the word "small." It is important to set small, realistic goals for yourself that you can successfully achieve, before trying to tackle more lofty goals.

Setting aside 5 minutes a day to go for a walk and being able to follow through with this (and building on this over time) might be more helpful than planning to set aside an hour and giving up because you find this too challenging.

> *Examples:* Leroy will say no to volunteering to organize the upcoming holiday party at work.
>
> Jessica will set aside 30 minutes today to turn off all phones, leave unfinished chores, and play with her children.
>
> Lynne will make a point of initiating one conversation at work in the next day with a coworker who sits near her.
>
> Sapir will spend 5 minutes on Monday sitting in his backyard before work, listening to and watching the birds. On Wednesday of this week he will spend 5 minutes before bed listening to a sounds of nature meditation.

WEEKLY REFLECTION

This week I am noticing what is most important to me in many areas of my life.

♦   I am noticing what qualities I most want to cultivate in the areas of work, family, non-family relationships, health, and personal time.

♦   I am becoming more aware of what gets in the way of living the valued, meaningful life that I most want in these areas.

- As I become aware of these obstacles, I also become aware of a growing willingness inside of me to experience some discomfort if it means I can take actions that will allow me to live a more valued life.

- I can see small, action steps that I can take toward living out my values, and I am committed to taking a small step each day.

- I choose to focus on these important qualities I am cultivating in myself, and the accompanying behaviors that they invite, to act as a beacon of light in the darkness, to help guide me towards living the life that I want.

KEY SUMMARY POINTS

On any journey, it is easier to follow our path if we identify what is most important to us and why what we are doing matters.

- Identifying core qualities in multiple areas of our lives that we want to live by can provide us with motivation to take committed actions that will move our lives in line with what we most value, and therefore make our lives more meaningful.

- Often, we do things (consciously or unconsciously) to avoid experiencing uncomfortable feelings. This "experiential avoidance" can get in the way of taking actions that would make our lives more meaningful.

- When we have a clearer sense of the obstacles that are blocking us from living the life we want, we can better develop a plan to work around or through those obstacles.

- By stepping back and putting things into a larger perspective or context, we can better recognize what is truly most important, and what is more insignificant.

- Once we do this, we can commit to taking small, concrete actions that are in line with the qualities we most value in ourselves and in line with the life that we most want to live.

Week 2, Exercise 1

🔊)) **IDENTIFYING WHAT QUALITIES ARE MOST IMPORTANT IN YOUR DAY'S "WORK"**

Describe what personal qualities are most important in your day's work:

If you were living your life fully in this way:	What would it feel like?
	What would it look like? What would you be doing?
	What would you think to yourself?
How close (or far) are you from living these values?	
What roadblocks get in the way?	
Are there any emotions you are avoiding?	

©2017 Beth Kurland, Ph.D.

Week 2, Exercise 2

🔊 **IDENTIFYING WHAT QUALITIES ARE MOST IMPORTANT IN YOUR FAMILY RELATIONSHIPS**

What personal qualities do you most want to bring to your family relationships? What is most important to you?

If you were living your life fully in this way:	What would it feel like?
	What would it look like? What would you be doing?
	What would you think to yourself?
How close (or far) are you from living these values?	
What roadblocks get in the way?	
Are there any emotions you are avoiding?	

©2017 Beth Kurland, Ph.D.

Week 2, Exercise 3

IDENTIFYING WHAT IS MOST IMPORTANT FOR YOUR PERSONAL HEALTH AND SELF-CARE

What is most important to you in the area of your life involving your health (physical, emotional, mental, and/or spiritual)?

If you were living your life fully in this way:	What would it feel like?
	What would it look like? What would you be doing?
	What would you think to yourself?
How close (or far) are you from living these values?	
What roadblocks get in the way?	
Are there any emotions you are avoiding?	

©2017 Beth Kurland, Ph.D.

Week 2, Exercise 4

 # IDENTIFYING WHAT QUALITIES ARE MOST IMPORTANT IN YOUR NON-FAMILY RELATIONSHIPS

What personal qualities do you most want to bring to your relationships with non-family members? What is most important to you?

If you were living your life fully in this way:	What would it feel like?
	What would it look like? What would you be doing?
	What would you think to yourself?
How close (or far) are you from living these values?	
What roadblocks get in the way?	
Are there any emotions you are avoiding?	

©2017 Beth Kurland, Ph.D.

Week 2, Exercise 5 **IDENTIFYING WHAT QUALITIES ARE MOST IMPORTANT IN YOUR PERSONAL TIME**	
What qualities are most important for you to cultivate when it comes to your personal time?	
If you were living your life fully in this way:	What would it feel like?
	What would it look like? What would you be doing?
	What would you think to yourself?
How close (or far) are you from living these values?	
What roadblocks get in the way?	
Are there any emotions you are avoiding?	

©2017 Beth Kurland, Ph.D.

	Week 2, Exercise 6
	PUTTING THINGS IN PERSPECTIVE TO WORK THROUGH ROADBLOCKS
List all of the roadblocks you previously identified:	
Now, choose one roadblock and answer the following questions:	1. If I were to work through this obstacle and face it head on, what might I do differently?
	2. Will there be any significant consequences in a week, or a month, or a year from now?
	3. Am I willing to work through this roadblock, even if it means feeling some discomfort, in order to live a more meaningful life? What might I gain by doing so?

©2017 Beth Kurland, Ph.D.

Week 2, Exercise 7

VISUALIZATION — PUTTING IT ALL TOGETHER

Write down any reflections from the meditation:

Week 2, Writing Activity
DEVELOPING AN ACTION PLAN

Look over the previous worksheets for this chapter.

Identify the qualities that are most important to you, and which ones you feel are furthest away from how you are currently living your life:

Using your responses to the above, write out some small, concrete action steps that you can take, starting right now, to bring this value (or values) into greater alignment in your life.

©2017 Beth Kurland, Ph.D.

WEEK THREE

MINDFULNESS

Building a Foundation For Well-Being by Anchoring Us in the Present Moment

"As I began to practice mindfulness, I was quite surprised to discover how much of the time my mind is anywhere but the present moment. Setting aside even just a few minutes each day to be present has helped me to pay more attention to simple things. When I do this, I notice I am more calm and grateful for the little moments." —COURTNEY

IN WEEK TWO, YOU HAD THE OPPORTUNITY to gain clarity about what is most important for you to live a life of meaning and value, and to discover in what ways you are and are not living that kind of life right now. You became aware of roadblocks that might be getting in your way, and you worked on developing a willingness to work with those roadblocks and take action, in order to have the life that you want. This week's chapter will help you learn a skill that you can use in all areas of your life and which is essential to live your life fully.

GOALS AND INTENTIONS FOR THIS WEEK

This week, you will learn about and practice cultivating mindfulness skills, which allow you to be more present in your life by living in this moment, right now. These skills lay the foundation for everything else that is to come. While you already have gotten a taste of this in previous weeks, you will now have the opportunity to delve deeper and to practice bringing mindfulness skills to your physical/body sensations, your thoughts, your emotions, and your behaviors. Learning how to do this will help you become less automatic, robotic, and reactive as you go through your day, and more conscious, aware, and present. As you will see in the two chapters that follow, when you are more aware of what you are thinking and feeling, and can learn to be present with your thoughts and emotions just as they are, you are less likely to be pulled away by negativity.

Why Is This Important?

As I briefly mentioned earlier, mindfulness is a particular way of paying attention. While the concept of mindfulness stems from Eastern psychological practices from more than 2,500 years ago, it has become popular in the western world in large part through the work of Jon Kabat-Zinn, Professor of Medicine Emeritus, founder of Mindfulness Based Stress Reduction (MBSR) and creator of the Stress Reduction Clinic at the University of Massachusetts Medical School. His definition of mindfulness is "paying attention in a particular way: on purpose, in the present moment, and nonjudgmentally" (Kabat-Zinn, 1994, p. 4).

Think about the last time you were present and attentive in this way. Perhaps it was when you were walking in the woods, playing with a child, laughing with a friend, doing something you love, eating a delicious dessert, listening to someone you care about, crying deeply over a loss in a way that gave you the space to be present with your sadness. To get a better understanding of mindfulness, it is helpful to look at what it is not. Imagine walking in the woods but instead of seeing the trees, you are worrying about how to pay your bills; or while playing a board game with your child, you are thinking about how angry you are at your boss and formulating the mean things you wish you could say to him/her; or while you are listening to a friend talk, you are thinking to yourself "I wonder if she thinks this scarf I have on looks stupid"; or "I can't believe she is going on and on about this topic again"; or while eating dessert you don't even notice the flavors you are eating because you are lost in thought or "somewhere else"; or while you are crying you tell yourself, "What is wrong with me, I should be over this by now! Those are all examples of what mindfulness is NOT.

The Benefits of Mindfulness

From these examples, I am sure you can appreciate that when we are mindful, our lives are more rich and meaningful. By making contact with what is right here and now in front of us, we have more access to the day-to-day joys of life, we experience greater ease and calmness, and we also have the space to feel our painful emotions as they arise, and work through them with compassion and ultimately acceptance. (More about that in Week Five.)

Mindfulness, when practiced regularly, has been shown to reduce levels of anxiety, depression, and stress in significant ways (Goyal et al., 2014). In addition to the emotional benefits of mindfulness, there are a substantial number of documented physical benefits of practicing mindfulness. Just as perceived stress can trigger high sympathetic nervous system activity and the fight-or-flight response, there is an opposite response in our bodies that is activated when we are relaxed. This is referred to as the "relaxation response" (Benson & Klipper, 2000).

One of the benefits of practicing mindfulness is that it can help turn down our stress response and elicit the relaxation response (Benson & Proctor, 2010). The medical benefits of reducing our stress response and turning on our relaxation response are far reaching. It can have a profound effect on our ability to stay healthy and prevent illness, and the ability of our bodies to heal from diseases and illnesses (Benson & Proctor, 2010; Rankin, 2013). Neuroscientist Dr. Richard Davidson's groundbreaking research at the University of Wisconsin-Madison has demonstrated, for example, that meditation can reduce the expression of genes that promote inflammation (which is thought to underlie many diseases); and even more exciting, that even just one day of intensive meditation practice can show changes in gene expression; two weeks of 30-minute compassion meditation can show changes in behavior and brain function, and even one and a half hours of mindfulness meditation practice can change the structure of the brain (Ricard et al., 2014). In addition, practicing mindfulness has been shown to increase gray matter in the brain and reduce cortical thinning, improve immune functioning, reduce pain levels, improve sleep, improve memory, and help slow cell death by increasing *telomerase* (the protective caps on chromosomes) (Hanson & Mendius, 2009; Siegel, 2010).

The Challenge of Being Mindful

If mindfulness is so good for us, why is it so difficult to do? If you think of the examples of what mindfulness is not, you may notice that much of your own behavior falls into the NOT mindful category much of the time. We can thank our evolutionary inheritance for this. As Ronald Siegel so eloquently writes about in his book, *The Mindfulness Solution* (2010), while we have inherited the more primitive, reactive part of our brain that we discussed in Week One, we also have evolved a higher "thinking" part of our brain that distinguishes us from other animals. This has allowed us to create, invent, build, and develop amazing technological advances and solve many complex problems. However, it is almost as if we don't know how to turn this thinking part of our brain off much of the time, and that is where we run into problems with being mindful (Siegel, 2010). In this way, our thinking is both a blessing and curse, so to speak.

To share an example similar to what Dr. Siegel writes about in his book (2010), imagine a squirrel or turtle or deer outside in the yard: do you think they spend their time thinking about what they are going to do a year from now when their babies are grown or how they are going to save up enough material for a nicer house next year, or worrying about whether that fox is going to come around next week, or ruminating about how their neighbor ate too much of their food yesterday, or concerning themselves with whether the other animals will think that the color of their fur or shell is unattractive? Only humans have the good fortune of those kinds of thoughts (Siegel, 2010). And when you begin to pay attention, you may realize that we have this sort of running commentary in our heads all day long, and that being "in our heads" takes us away from being present in the moment.

While we can't turn our thought stream off, mindfulness can help us become more aware of this constant chatter in our heads so that it doesn't pull us away from the present moment. With practice, we can redirect our attention gently and compassionately back to the present moment, even as the mind chatter drifts into the background. In addition, mindfulness can help us learn to be more present with the emotions arising within us, in a compassionate, nonjudgmental, and accepting way, so that we are not as swept away and reactive to our emotions. Mindfulness can help us become more compassionate towards ourselves and others through our nonjudgmental awareness; it can help decrease anxiety, stress and depression by helping us not to get pulled into thoughts of past hurts and future *what ifs*; and it can give us greater control over our behavior by helping us step out of our habitual, reactive, and automatic patterns of being.

Formal and Informal Mindfulness Practice

We can bring this kind of mindful attention to any and all moments in our day, in an "informal" way—by attending mindfully as we are going about our routine activities of life (getting dressed, showering, eating, talking with others, folding laundry, driving, participating in a hobby, sitting in a meeting, playing with a child, etc.). We can also practice being mindful in a more "formal" way, by setting aside a specified period of time and picking an object of focus (such as our breathing) and bringing our full, mindful attention to it over and over, continually redirecting our attention back to the breath even as our thoughts try to pull us away. This more "formal" practice is often referred to as mindfulness meditation. There are benefits to both formal and informal practice. In an interview with Maria Shriver on NBC News, Dr. Richard Davidson mentions the importance of informal mindfulness practice, saying "Being distracted exacts a cost on our well-being . . . If we become more mindful of our everyday activities, we can learn well-being and become happier" (Davidson, 2014).

In either formal or informal practice, by becoming an observer of our thoughts, feelings, and sensations (as we began to explore in Week One) in a nonjudgmental, accepting, and purposefully aware way, we develop the ability to be less pulled away by them and more able to bring our attention to the here and now. This helps us to decrease the "suffering" that we create by the thinking in our own heads (e.g., worrying about things that often never happen), and helps to increase our enjoyment of the here and now moments of our lives.

To illustrate mindfulness, imagine that I decide to practice being mindful of my breathing for 10 minutes. My mind might go something like this: "Breathing in, breathing out, breathing in, ooh my arm really itches, I wonder if I got poison ivy from walking in the woods the other day, oh wait—back to the breath, breathing in, breathing out, breathing in, I wonder if I am doing this right? Maybe I'm doing this wrong—wait, don't judge myself, there is no right or wrong, just breathing in, breathing out, breathe in, breathe out, I think I forgot to buy milk, breathe in, breathe out, and so on. It is natural for the mind to wander—a lot—but the task is to observe, notice, and compassionately redirect your attention back to this moment, whether you are choosing to focus on your breathing in a more formal practice, or to focus on whatever you are doing right now in your day. In Week One we began to experience and practice this mindful attention as it relates to the stress we experience in our lives. Here we will widen our scope of awareness to every day moments of our lives. Week Four will focus more in depth on working with our thoughts, and in Week Five we will focus on working with our challenging emotions in mindful ways.

Like building a house by starting with a strong foundation, this book is intended to help you build your strong foundation, step by step. In the following exercises, we will have the opportunity to explore more about how to be mindful. We will then be able to develop these skills in the forthcoming weeks to help keep us from being pulled away by strong negative thoughts and emotions.

While we have a thinking brain that can make it a challenge to practice mindfulness, we are also blessed with an amazing body that can see, hear, smell, touch, and taste things in our world through all of our senses. It turns out that these senses can act as a secret key to give us access to this gift called the present. When we are experiencing the world through our bodies and our many senses, we are not lost in our heads, and this helps us make contact with and live in the present moment.

In the following exercises, we will practice ways of being more present in our lives by bringing our moment-to-moment awareness into our bodies and senses. As in all of the exercises in this book, be mindful of moving through each of these exercises at whatever pace works best for you and of spending more than one day on any exercise you choose. At the end of each chapter, you will have the opportunity to practice integrating all of the exercises from that chapter.

 **Exercise One**

Mindful Breathing and Noticing Thoughts

It turns out that our breathing is a wonderful way to bring us into the present moment when we choose to turn our attention to it. While we often don't pay attention to our breath, it is *always* there for us, a constant on which we can always depend. By focusing on our breathing, we can bring our awareness into our bodies and into the here and now. This exercise will also give you practice in learning to observe and let go of the constant stream of thoughts that arise in your mind. (Whether you are a complete novice to this, or an expert meditator, this exercise can be done daily to train the mind to be more present.)

Today's exercise involves setting aside 10 minutes to focus on your breathing. I suggest you set a timer or preferably use a mindfulness bell (apps are available for most cell phones). You may follow the instructions here, or use the audio for this exercise.

Begin by getting into a comfortable seated position where you can remain uninterrupted for 10 minutes. Start to bring your attention to your breathing, noticing each inhalation, and each exhalation. It is likely that very quickly your mind will start to generate thoughts—often seemingly nonstop. This is normal so don't be discouraged. The idea is that there is no right or wrong here; it is all about learning to be present with what is. There is no goal, nothing to achieve. If striving or judgments arise, see if you can let these go.

Take the role of an observer and acknowledge each thought as it comes into your awareness, and then gently guide yourself back to your breathing. When your thoughts arise it can be helpful to use a visual image to allow them to pass by as you bring your attention back to your breathing. Some common images are: seeing your thoughts as clouds passing by in the sky, imagining each thought as a leaf floating down a stream (Hayes & Smith, 2005), or putting each thought on a train and watching the train disappear in the distance as you turn your attention back to breathing.

With each breath, notice the sensation of it, the rhythm and feel of it, the rise and fall, the pace, the fullness or shallowness of it. Notice where in your body you are aware of your breath: perhaps in your chest, your belly, your nose, or somewhere else in your body.

Don't worry about trying to change anything, just let it be as it is. As thoughts arise, gently notice them, perhaps noting what kind of thoughts they are (e.g., worries, to do's, planning, ruminating and judging.), and then redirect your attention back to your breathing. It is common to have thoughts about whether you are doing this right, about boredom, about whether this is "working." Notice the tendency of your mind to judge and evaluate, then simply return to the breath. Know that observing your experience, whatever its form, is the goal, not trying to stop your thoughts.

Stay with each breath cycle as long as you can, noticing the peak of each inhalation and the valley of each exhalation. Continue until 10 minutes have passed, or longer if you would like. Afterwards, record on your worksheet what you observed about this experience.

> *Example*: Courtney had never done any mindful breathing before and found it challenging and interesting. She noticed her tendency to quickly judge herself with thoughts such as "my mind has wandered off again" and her striving to "get it right." She tried to take these thoughts lightly, and found it helpful to imagine putting each thought on a train and watching it move toward the horizon to not get hooked by these thoughts. Later during the day, she was surprised to notice how often she had a running mental commentary of judgments of her behavior, similar to what she noticed during the exercise.

EXERCISE TWO

Mindfulness through the Senses

Today is an opportunity to practice mindfulness using your five senses as you go about your day.

Pick at least three daily routines (or more if you wish) and bring your awareness to as many of your five senses as you can while you are engaging in that activity. Some possible activities might include brushing your teeth, taking a shower, eating, driving, washing dishes or folding laundry. If you were taking a shower, for example, you might pay attention to the feeling of the water on your skin, the sensation of your fingers on your scalp as you wash your hair, the smell of the soap and shampoo, the sound of the water hitting the shower floor, the color of the soap and the way it makes suds in your hand.

When your mind wanders off, similar to the breathing exercise above, you will gently redirect it back to the task at hand and to the sensory information that your body is experiencing at that moment.

> *Example*: Since Miranda had noticed from the exercises in Week One that she tended to engage in mindless eating, she decided to use eating as one of her mindful activities. Instead of eating on the run or in front of the TV, she made it a point to eat at the table, with no other distractions. She was amazed by the experience of truly tasting her food, chewing it slowly, and savoring each bite. She noticed flavors, textures, and aromas to which she usually paid no attention. She experienced pleasure in this meal, and was much more aware of her body's signal of when she was full, something she usually missed when engrossed in other distractions during eating.

 **EXERCISE THREE**

Mindfulness through Movement

This exercise involves setting aside 10 minutes for mindfulness while moving, either in the form of slow walking, gentle stretching, or yoga (if you are familiar). Alternatively, you could do this exercise by lying down and stretching and releasing different body parts, or by simply scanning your body from head to toe. The idea is to fully inhabit your body and bring your awareness to what it feels like to be in your body.

The focus of your awareness is on any and all sensations within your body, moment to moment. If you decide to do the exercise while walking, you could take off your shoes and walk barefoot to increase the sensations on the bottoms of your feet. If walking—either with shoes or without—focus on the sensations of each step: your foot making contact with the earth, the feeling of your joints bending and your muscles supporting you, the pressure of your feet on the ground and the feeling of your upper limbs moving through the air.

If you are lying down, pick one part of your body to start with, such as your feet, and focus on the sensations in your feet. You might choose to stretch and flex your foot to further increase the sensations there. Then move up to your lower legs and so forth. As with the previous exercises, as your mind wanders, gently bring it back to the present moment and into the sensations within your body.

Be sure to record your observations on the worksheet after you complete the exercise.

Example: Karen practiced mindful walking. She was used to living her life at a fairly hectic pace, so walking slowly like this felt new and challenging for her, yet at the same time calming. She noticed that her mind kept jumping to thoughts like "there is so much I should be doing right now," but she imagined these thoughts as sand at the beach being washed away by the waves as she brought her attention back to the sensations in her feet. She felt calmer afterwards, and realized the benefits of mindfully slowing down.

Example: Byron practiced scanning his body while lying in bed in the morning before work. He had recently strained his back and found that almost immediately upon starting this exercise, his mind focused on thoughts such as "I bet my back is going to hurt again today. I was really looking forward to playing golf this weekend, I am going to be so mad if I can't play." When he noticed this happening he would redirect his attention back to whatever body part he was focusing on, but was intrigued by how quickly his mind would jump to thoughts about his back and speculations about pain in the week ahead. He also noticed that having these thoughts alone caused his muscles to tighten. When he directed his attention to his back in a mindful way, he was surprised that the sensations of discomfort were relatively mild compared to what he had worked himself up to expect.

EXERCISE FOUR

Mindful Listening

Today your task is to find an opportunity during the day to practice being present while listening to another person talk. In this exercise, the focus of your attention is on another person: listening intently to their words, noticing their nonverbal body language, facial expressions, and emotions, and doing so in an open, nonjudgmental way. If you want, you can practice this multiple times throughout the day with different conversations. When your mind begins to wander off, see if you can catch yourself and bring your focus back to listening.

Notice how this feels in your body—does your body feel open and receptive, tense, closed off? Notice your own posture and nonverbal "body language" as you listen. Record your observations on your worksheet.

> *Example*: Jessica, who had identified wanting to be more present with her children, decided to try this exercise with her five-year-old son, who loved to talk nonstop. When he started to tell her a story about his stuffed animals, she chose to stop what she was doing and give him her full, undivided attention. She listened to his words, his excited tone, and noticed how his body was bursting with expression. At first, she noticed her own body feeling slightly tense, with thoughts drifting to her half-written email, but she was able to refocus her attention on her son and felt an increasing openness in her own body, and a warm feeling in her heart. She realized how often she is only "half-listening" when her children talk to her while she is involved in doing activities around the house.

> *Example*: Russell, as you may recall from the previous week, identified that one of the qualities he valued was being respectful with his employees at work, so he decided to try this exercise at work. When one of his employees started telling him about a mistake he had made, Russell decided to try and listen mindfully without being immediately reactive. He realized how much tension he had in his body as the employee began to speak, and how his first reaction was to tense up

and shut down. In addition, he noticed how quickly he started having judgmental thoughts without really hearing this person out. He tried to see these thoughts passing like clouds in the sky (e.g., "what is wrong with him"; "that was stupid") so that he could truly hear what was being said. He also noticed that the employee was anxious and clearly felt concerned about the matter. When Russell noticed this, it helped him to feel more empathy in his own body.

EXERCISE FIVE

Mindful Relating/Connecting

This exercise is an extension of the previous one. Instead of just focusing on listening mindfully to someone else, today, you will focus your awareness on how you initiate and participate in conversations and interactions. Pick at least one interaction to use for this exercise, but preferably more than one. Focus your attention within yourself before you initiate a conversation, and then pay mindful attention throughout the interaction to yourself as well as the other person. Be aware of what you are experiencing in your body; be aware of your thoughts, your emotions, and your words and how they are spoken. In addition, try to listen mindfully as practiced previously.

Write down your observations on your worksheet.

Example: Maya had noticed from an exercise in Week One that her stress response was triggered during conversations with her husband about finances. She needed to talk with him about the week's budget so she chose to use this as an opportunity to practice mindfulness in interaction. Before she even entered the room where he sat, she noticed that her body had become very tense. Instead of storming into the room, she decided to take a few moments to breath, which helped to relax her muscles. She was very aware of how she walked into the room, and her tone of voice when she asked her husband whether he had time to talk. She made an effort to pay attention to what her husband said instead of turning to a ready response already in her head beforehand. She noticed her tendency to start making judgments without having all of the information. What Maya was most aware of was how different this felt from her usual way of interacting with her husband on financial issues. She was able to observe herself and adjust her behavior to listen more openly and express her words in a way her husband was more likely to hear.

EXERCISE SIX

Observing Emotions as a Focus of Awareness

This next exercise will combine mindfully listening to a piece of music with being mindful of your emotions as your object of attention. You will need to set aside a few minutes when you can listen to a piece of music uninterrupted (and not while driving). Choose a song or piece of music that will evoke an emotional response. It could be a piece of music you find inspirational; one that moves you; reminds you of someone you used to know, brings back a meaningful time in your life, makes you feel uplifted or is humorous.

Play the music at least once, but preferably twice, so you can fully experience it. As you listen, turn your awareness to the emotions it evokes in you, and see if you can make these the focus of your attention for several minutes. Notice how the emotion is experienced in your body, where you feel it, and what sensations are associated with it. Also notice any memories that may be associated with this emotion.

As your mind fills with other thoughts, gently redirect yourself back to experiencing your feelings, whatever they might be, in your body. See if you can allow yourself to be with whatever emotion is present without judging yourself and without pushing it away.

Write down your observations on your worksheet.

Example: Bernie chose to listen to one of his favorite songs from high school, which had sentimental value for him. The song made him think fondly of his closest childhood friends and also remember one of those friends who died several years ago. As Bernie immersed himself in the song, he noticed at first a warm feeling in his body and a smile on his face as he thought of this close group of boys, and their many adventures. As he stayed with the feelings in his body, he noticed a sadness that started in the pit of his stomach and spread to his heart. He caught himself moments later thinking about work, and realized how hard it was for him to stay with the sadness. He started to get upset with himself for feeling sad, then tried to let go of this judgment and put his attention back on the feeling in his body. Tears welled up in his eyes. Despite the inclination to distract himself, he turned again toward the sadness and simply noticed it in his body. Afterwards Bernie noted how hard it was to allow himself to feel sad, and yet how doing so in this exercise helped show him that this emotion need not be avoided.

EXERCISE SEVEN

Being Mindful throughout the Day

In this exercise feel free to follow along here or use the guided audio. Begin by getting into a comfortable position where you can sit for at least 5 minutes, preferably at the beginning of the day.

Turn your awareness to your breathing and take several breaths, in and out, following each inhalation and exhalation. Notice your breathing in this moment, without needing to change it in any way.

As thoughts arise in your mind unrelated to this exercise, see if you can gently let them go and bring your focus back. When you are ready, take some time to imagine yourself going through your day and week being very mindful and present. You could imagine watching these scenes unfold on a movie or TV screen in front of you.

Notice what it looks like to be living your life in this way. What kind of things do you do when you are mindful?

- How do you speak and interact with others?
- How does it feel in your body to be living mindfully?

Take some time to really feel this in your body and let this feeling become vivid and familiar to you. See yourself going through your daily routines with mindful awareness. Notice what you do to bring yourself back to the present when your mind gets caught up in thought. Notice how being mindful might help you to move toward embodying the qualities that are most important to you in the different areas of your life that we explored in Week Two. Imagine how you will feel interacting with others when you bring mindfulness into your life.

As you go about your day today, take note of how close you are to having the kind of mindful day that you envisioned.

Note on your worksheet all the ways that you were mindful that you would not have been before. Also make note of any obstacles or challenges to being mindful, without judging yourself for this.

Example: Russell was able to visualize with some clarity what it would feel and look like to go through his day with more mindful attention. While his actual day did not quite match what he envisioned, he was struck by the small moments throughout his day when he was able to be present, and how this made a difference to his state of mind and mood. For example, in the shower he had a few minutes where he mindfully enjoyed the feeling of the water falling on his body, instead of getting lost in thoughts anticipating stressors at work. When he said goodbye to his wife, he lingered in and enjoyed their embrace, when normally he would rush out the door hardly remembering this moment. While walking into his building, he parked farther away than usual so that he could take those few minutes to enjoy the fresh air and feeling of sunshine on his face. At work he was more aware of listening to others with more openness and non-judgment.

WRITING ACTIVITY
MINDFULNESS ACTION PLAN

Look through all your worksheets from this week and notice what you learned about yourself. Take note of where you have been able to be more mindful, what helped you do this, and what challenged you most about being present. Notice any connections between this week's exercises and previous weeks. Then make an action plan identifying what you will do going forward to practice being more mindful each day.

Pick one or two small, specific, concrete actions to which you can commit and follow through with on a daily basis.

Examples: Miranda decided that she would make it a point to eat lunch away from her computer, so that she could pay more attention to the experience of eating. She set an intention for herself to eat mindfully during each workday lunch, paying attention to her food as well as the signals from her body.

Russell chose to practice mindful listening in the workplace. Whenever an employee started speaking to him he was going to try to attend to what they were saying in a mindful manner, by really listening to what they said before jumping in with his own reactions.

Karen decided that she would set aside a minimum of 5 minutes every day to "slow down" in some way by either doing mindful breathing, mindful walking, or some yoga poses. In addition, she decided that she would make a point of starting the day by brushing her teeth with mindful attention, as a way of practicing being present. She hoped to expand this over time to other daily routines, but she wanted to start with something small that she knew she could follow through with.

WEEKLY REFLECTION

Today I remind myself
to be fully present
and inhabit each moment
with all of my senses.

I remind myself
to listen from a place of
presence
and non-judgment
and compassion.

When I interact with others
I will practice being aware
of what I am experiencing within

and what is happening to the other person
so that I may choose actions
that are most in line with how I want to be.

I choose to practice
training my mind
to return
again and again
to this precious moment
of now.

KEY SUMMARY POINTS

- Mindfulness is simply a way of paying attention, with non-judgment and awareness of this moment right here and now.

- While it seems so simple, our minds tend to generate a constant stream of thoughts (often outside of our awareness) that pull us away repeatedly from the present moment so that we get "lost in our thinking." While there are times when our thinking is vital to a task at hand, there are many times when our thoughts are not helpful to what we are doing in the moment.

- It takes continual practice to train our minds to come back to the present moment. It is very normal to have to bring our attention back over and over to the present, even multiple times within a minute.

- It is important to notice any judgments you may have about yourself and this process of being mindful (e.g., "I'm not doing it right") so that you can practice letting these go and becoming more compassionate towards yourself.

- Our bodies and our senses are very helpful in assisting us to experience the present. By bringing awareness to physical sensations in our bodies and to sensory input it is as if we are given a key to step into the present moment.

🔊))) Week 3, Exercise 1
MINDFUL BREATHING AND NOTICING THOUGHTS

List what you practiced:

Describe any observations from this practice:

How might you use this in your day:

©2017 Beth Kurland, Ph.D.

Week 3, Exercise 2
MINDFULNESS THROUGH THE SENSES

List what you practiced:

Describe any observations from this practice:

How might you use this in your day:

©2017 Beth Kurland, Ph.D.

Week 3, Exercise 3

🔊))) **MINDFULNESS THROUGH MOVEMENT**

List what you practiced:

Describe any observations from this practice:

How might you use this in your day:

©2017 Beth Kurland, Ph.D.

Week 3, Exercise 4
MINDFUL LISTENING

List what you practiced:

Describe any observations from this practice:

How might you use this in your day:

Week 3, Exercise 5
MINDFUL RELATING/CONNECTING

List what you practiced:

Describe any observations from this practice:

How might you use this in your day:

Week 3, Exercise 6

OBSERVING EMOTIONS AS A FOCUS OF AWARENESS

List what you practiced:

Describe any observations from this practice:

How might you use this in your day:

Week 3, Exercise 7

🔊 BEING MINDFUL THROUGHOUT THE DAY

Observations from this visualization exercise:

List all of the ways that you were mindful today:

Obstacles/challenges that arose to being mindful:

©2017 Beth Kurland, Ph.D.

Week 3, Writing Activity
MINDFULNESS ACTION PLAN

Looking through all of the worksheets from this chapter:

What did you learn about yourself?

Where have you been most mindful? What was most helpful to encourage this?

What challenges arose to being mindful?

Mindfulness Action Plan:

1.

2.

©2017 Beth Kurland, Ph.D.

Week Four

NEGATIVE THINKING

How It Pulls Us Into a Downward Spiral & What to Do About It

"I was shocked when I really stopped and listened to what I was saying to myself all day long. If anyone ever spoke to me like that I would be appalled, yet that voice is in my head day in and out. Having tools to catch this negativity and feed myself a healthier diet of positive thoughts has brought more ease into my day." —Tina

In Week One, you began noticing how your thinking can contribute to your stress reactions (for example, how your perceptions and interpretations of situations can increase or decrease your stress). In Week Three, you learned about what mindfulness is, and you practiced being mindful with physical body sensations, thoughts, emotions, and in your interactions with others. You have the awareness now to catch yourself more often when you are NOT being mindful, and this will become a very powerful tool in your life. You also likely realized how simple yet challenging it is to stay in the present moment. This is a continual work in progress, so be careful not to be hard on yourself if you find it difficult. Awareness is the key to making small changes towards transformation one day at a time, and your next step on this journey is to bring greater awareness to your thoughts.

GOALS AND INTENTIONS FOR THIS WEEK

This week, you will learn how your thoughts can pull you into a negativity trap that can affect your body, emotions, and behaviors. You will notice ways that you may feed yourself an unhealthy diet of negative thoughts, and you will have the opportunity to use mindfulness and other tools to stop yourself from getting pulled into this negative-thinking spiral.

Why Is This Important?

We are all probably aware of how the "diet" we feed ourselves can impact our bodies and health. When we choose to eat healthy foods, this has positive consequences for our health and well-being. What we may not recognize is the tendency for most of us to feed ourselves a daily "diet" of negative thoughts, and the impact this has on our bodies, emotions, and actions. The field of Cognitive-Behavioral Therapy teaches us that not only do our negative thoughts often fall below the surface of our awareness, but they also can quickly spiral us downward once we are caught in this negative thought stream. The problem is that much of the time we do not recognize the occurrence of our negative thoughts, and the impact they have on us.

If we are not mindful, our thoughts have a way of lurking just below our field of awareness, in that place of automatic pilot and habitual thinking. If left unchecked, they can act like dominoes, one negative thought setting off the next. When this happens, it is not uncommon for our thinking to trigger negative emotions from experiences that have occurred in our past. Soon we may not only be dealing with the current situation, but unknowingly, with past hurts, wounds, and upsets, too (e.g., how many times have you been in an argument and verbalized thoughts such as "you *never* listen to me!" while thinking about all of the other times in your life that you may have felt misunderstood). It is also common for our negative thinking to become irrational. We can get pulled into thought traps, such as seeing things as "all or nothing" (look for the words "always" and "never" in your thinking) and "black or white," when in fact there are usually "grays" that we miss. We also have a tendency to catastrophize and exaggerate, seeing the worst in a situation, when in fact that is not the most accurate or realistic interpretation. Our thinking can become distorted in other ways, such as forecasting negative events that may never occur, over generalizing, jumping to conclusions, or taking things personally. It is hard for us to examine issues or events in a helpful or realistic way when we are caught in this downward spiral of negativity.

A Closer Look at the Negativity Spiral

Let's take a look at how this can happen, and the impact of negative thinking on one's emotions, body, and behavior. Kelsey is getting ready to go to a college party and starts thinking thoughts such as "I wonder if I am going to have fun." Soon other thoughts come into her head such as "what if people think I'm a bore," and "nobody is going to want to hang out with me." Her mind quickly moves from there to thoughts of previous high school parties at which she felt left out, which triggers further thoughts such as "nobody likes me" and "I'm such a loser." These thoughts in turn trigger negative emotions and stress in her body, turning on the stress response and releasing stress chemicals into her bloodstream. When she arrives at the party, she is tense and on alert. When no one immediately greets her, she quickly interprets this as proof that no one wants to be around her, and that she must be unlikeable. When she sees several people across the room talking to one another and glancing briefly over at her, she immediately assumes they are talking about her. These thoughts, and the accompanying negative emotions, cause her to be more isolative rather than friendly. People at the party may in fact begin to "read" her isolation as a desire to be left alone. They may not approach her as readily, not because they don't like her, but because she seems like she wants some space. This isolation further reinforces her negative thinking that no one likes her.

Examining this example further, one can see the tendency for Kelsey's negative thinking to be irrational, inaccurate, and extreme. Kelsey starts off wondering if she will have fun, but quickly spirals to a conclusion that no one will like her and thinking of herself as a loser. Her thinking is blown out of proportion, and all-or-nothing in nature. In addition, her mind focuses on times in her past when she felt left out, and this pulls her further into a downward spiral. This in turn affects her body (her cells become bathed in stress chemicals, which, if this occurs on a chronic basis, can take a negative toll on her body); she becomes emotionally upset, and, in turn she behaves in ways that are not conducive to meeting people and making friends.

How Mindful Awareness Can Help

If Kelsey had been able to be more mindful and aware of her negative thoughts, and able to observe them without getting swept away by them (the skills we started practicing in previous weeks), she may have been able to catch herself and put things in perspective. She may have recognized the inaccuracy of the statement that "no one" likes her, and instead reminded herself that she does have several good, close friends. She may have acknowledged her tendency to be shy, rather than calling herself a "loser." And she might have become aware that what happened in high school had its own set of circumstances and was not relevant to what was happening now at this college party. In turn, if the negative thinking had not been foremost in Kelsey's mind, she might have been more willing to initiate conversations with others at the party, rather than isolating herself and creating a self-fulfilling prophesy.

Sometimes our negative thinking can be more subtle than the example with Kelsey. Remember Barbara in Week One, who thinks to herself: "Oh god, I have a long day ahead of me. I have so much to do. It's gonna be a tough day." This kind of thinking can easily slip through the cracks of our awareness, yet it has a significant impact on how we set ourselves up to experience our day.

Distinguishing Helpful from Unhelpful Thinking

Our negative thinking may not always be irrational, but to focus on it may be unhelpful all the same. You may recall Winona (from Week One) who starts thinking about how stressful the weekend will be when her parents visit, thus experiencing that stress not only when her parents arrive, but also experiencing it in her mind well before the situation occurs. (In this case, it may be that her parents are demanding, and their visits usually lead to conflict and tension, but it does no good for Winona to live this stress in her mind before it actually happens, when there is nothing she can do about it.)

This brings up another important point. As we explored in last week's chapter, our minds are constantly generating thoughts; sometimes those thoughts are useful, productive, creative, and essential for problem-solving, planning, and inventing. But sometimes our thinking actually takes us away from experiencing the present moment.

If Winona could stop and think about proactive strategies for addressing her concerns about her parents' visit (e.g., setting boundaries with them in advance by asking them not to undermine her parenting decisions), this could be an example of thinking that leads to a productive outcome. When we can recognize the difference between productive thinking, and negative, unhelpful thinking, we have more choice and power over how we react to our thoughts. When we can use our thinking in useful ways, and practice observing and letting negative, unhelpful thoughts pass, our lives flow more easily.

Another example of how negative thinking can enter our lives is in our perceptions and interpretations of events. Remember, most situations are not inherently stressful in and of themselves. It is our interpretation of a situation that creates or at least exacerbates the stress. While one person may perceive a boss as wonderful, another can perceive that same person as quite negative. While one person may experience a broken leg as devastating, another person could see it as an opportunity to slow down and focus on self-care activities. As a small example, think about the common tendency to say to yourself something like "it's so miserable and nasty outside!" on a cold or rainy day (I am writing as a long time New Englander). I remember verbalizing this thought myself one frigid and windy January day to my cousin, who responded that for him, the cold made him feel fully alive. This struck me as so simple yet profound, that a slight shift in our perception could completely change an experience. To this day when I am out in the cold I try to think about and appreciate the feeling of aliveness that the cold air brings. While that is a seemingly minor example, the small shifts in our thinking often add up over time to bring more positivity into our day-to-day lives.

The Power of Awareness and Choice

By simply recognizing our negative thinking, and, when relevant, the irrational nature of those thoughts, we create an opportunity to choose something different. Recall that we live with the evolutionary inheritance of a negativity bias; our brains are wired to see the threats and negatives in our environment, because this helped us survive as a species. We have to rewire our brains through conscious effort in order to experience more positives. We may not be able to stop the initial negative thoughts from coming into our minds, but we can choose whether we run with them and let them take over, or gently and compassionately turn the focus of our attention to other "truths" in our awareness, particularly ones that may be more accurate, realistic, and/or helpful.

A quote that I often share with my patients is one by Lee Ross: "Optimism is not about providing a recipe for self-deception. The world can be a horrible, cruel place; and at the same time, it can be wonderful and abundant. These are both truths. There is not a half-way point; there is only choosing which truth to put in your personal foreground." (Lyubomirsky 2008, p.111). We have a profound power to choose how we look at a situation. We may not be able to change certain circumstances in our lives, and we cannot necessarily stop our negative thoughts from arising initially, but we can choose where to focus our attention. An analogy I often share with my patients, taught to me many years ago, and one I have since come across by others (Fowler, 2014; Pasinski & Gould, 2011), is the idea of "changing the radio station." The broadcasts of various different radio stations exist in the atmosphere all the time, but what we choose to listen to depends on where we tune in. We can choose to tune into "negativity 101.5," which plays the same messages over and over again about all the things that are wrong with us and our lives, or we can allow those negative thoughts to drift into the background as we tune in to station "positivity 106.5." What I am NOT suggesting is some distorted version of Pollyanna where we say to ourselves that everything is great and wonderful, if it is not. But if someone loses a job, they can choose to focus on thoughts such as "economic times are hard," or "this job wasn't a good fit for my skill set," rather than "I'm a loser and no one will ever hire me." If someone struggles with social anxiety they can choose to focus on thoughts such as "I am uncomfortable in new social situations, but I know once people get to know me I have a lot to offer as a friend," instead of "everyone dislikes me and I'll never make friends!"

When we increase our awareness of our negative thinking through mindfulness, this offers us several options:

1. We can simply observe and notice our negative thoughts and try to watch them pass by in a mindful fashion without getting pulled by them into a downward spiral;

2. We can notice and replace our distorted, unrealistic thoughts with ones that are more accurate, realistic, and helpful;

3. We can choose where we focus our attention and allow the negative thoughts to drift to the background while we put our attention on the present moment and more helpful, affirming thoughts in our personal foreground.

In the exercises that follow, you will have an opportunity to practice cultivating these skills. Before doing this, I want to mention one thing about ruminating thoughts.

Sometimes negative thoughts can be so intense that they become "stuck" in an endless loop in our minds. They can seem to take over, despite our effort to use strategies to put them in the background. When that happens, patients often say to me "the only thing that works is for me to distract myself." One patient said that her "distraction" is going into her backyard shed and doing carpentry. Another patient told me her "distraction" is taking her dog for a walk in the woods. Another described playing with her baby to help shift away from the ruminating thoughts. I like to reframe this notion of "distraction"; the activities that they are engaging in are not the distraction; instead it is the negative thoughts that are the distraction pulling them away from the present moment. Choosing activities to focus on in a mindful way, helps to release the thought distractions and bring us back to what is happening here and now before us. So when negative thoughts are particularly intense, engaging in an enjoyable activity in a mindful way can be helpful to bring oneself back into one's life and out of one's head.

EXERCISE ONE

Catching Your Negative Thoughts, Big and Small

The purpose of this exercise is to become more adept at noticing your negative thinking and its impact on you, in order to build on the skills we have been working on in the preceding weeks. Also, you will practice observing your thoughts without getting pulled away by them.

As you go about your day today, see if you can observe your own thinking, as if you were watching subtitles on a movie screen. At the first sign of any negative thinking, STOP and notice what you are saying to yourself. Make note of whether it is irrational or distorted in some way (we will do more with this in the next exercise). Notice how it feels in your body when you think these thoughts. See if you can observe these thoughts nonjudgmentally, in a similar way to exercises in the previous week's chapter. Perhaps you can imagine the thought passing by like a cloud in the sky, or as a leaf floating down the stream, or getting washed away by the ocean waves. (These are techniques from Acceptance and Commitment Therapy referred to as thought diffusion strategies.) You could also say to yourself "this is just a thought created by my mind, and nothing more."

Then bring your awareness back to the task at hand. If you can't let the thought go, see if you can simply be with it, and the accompanying emotions, without getting pulled into a downward spiral. Focus your awareness on your breathing to help you do this.

Another way to catch negative thinking is to observe when negative moods arise, because they often go hand in hand. Pay attention to your mood today and when you notice your mood souring, stop and notice: what are you thinking right now? How are your thoughts contributing to your mood? How are they affecting your body? How are they affecting your behavior? Record your negative thoughts on your worksheet, along with any observations.

Example: Tina was surprised how often she caught herself engaged in negative thinking. Multiple times throughout the day, she noticed that she would say to herself, "I'm such an idiot," or "I'm so stupid," for minor things that she did. It struck her that she would never talk to anyone else like this, yet she talked to herself like this often. She noticed that when she did this, she experienced a heaviness in her body. At one point in the day she found herself lost in thought. When she stopped to pay attention, she realized she was thinking about the new assignment she got at work, and was saying to herself, "This is awful. How am I going to have time to take this on? I'll never be able to do a good job with this."

Tina became aware of how tense her body felt as she was thinking these things. When she realized she was caught up in these thoughts she tried to let them pass by without letting them pull her in further. She noticed the tendency for one negative thought to lead to another, more intense one, and so on. Stopping and focusing on her breathing for a few minutes was helpful in this regard. She imagined her thoughts written on helium balloons that she released and watched drift away in the sky.

Afterwards, she still noticed the negative thoughts coming, but she had more of a sense of watching them rather than being completely swallowed by them.

Example: Caleb had an easier time identifying his negative thinking when he was able to notice his mood fluctuations throughout the day. In the morning, he noticed himself getting agitated. The thoughts he discovered were, "Oh it's

Monday. The traffic is gonna be hell today. I'll bet work is gonna be nonstop too, and then I have to stop at my brother's house to help him out. This day is gonna be endless." Later, he found himself becoming irritable and angry at his ten-year-old son, who had forgotten to hand in a homework assignment.

When Caleb stopped to notice his accompanying thoughts, he caught himself thinking, "I can't believe he forgot to turn this in. This isn't the first time. This is terrible. How is he going to manage in life? How is he going to get through school being this irresponsible?" Later, when his wife came home and forgot to bring a package that he had requested, he noticed feeling agitated and thinking, "She always does this. Why can't she remember one simple thing? If she really cared about me, she would have remembered this."

For each of these situations, Caleb was able to pause and recognize his thinking was exaggerated and extreme. This realization helped take the intensity out of it, although he still found himself pulled in by the thoughts. His awareness helped stop him from getting pulled in any deeper than he already was, however, and he found it helpful to imagine his thoughts as bubbles in a cartoon.

EXERCISE TWO

Working with Irrational Thoughts

Today you will have a chance to practice working more specifically with any irrational thoughts that you "catch." You can do this by using either your thought record from yesterday, or by keeping track of negative thoughts that arise today. For each of the negative thoughts that you identify, ask yourself the following questions:

- Am I making something bigger or worse than it actually is?
- Am I jumping to conclusions about something without evidence to support it?
- Am I thinking in extremes, and is there perhaps a more accurate middle ground?
- Am I predicting or forecasting into the future?
- What evidence do I have that this is a true statement?
- Am I fundamentally doing all right in this moment, right here and now?

After going through these questions, take a moment to rewrite your thought, making it more accurate, realistic or true, if appropriate. Make sure not to say anything that does not feel true (e.g., "everything is going to work out great" if you don't believe this). This is not about giving yourself a pep talk; this is about making your thoughts more accurate.

Tip: Pay close attention to the specific language that you use, because our choice of language can directly affect how we feel. For example, notice the difference between these two thoughts and how it makes you feel to say these statements out loud: "I'm such a loser and I'm so stupid" versus "I'm upset with myself that I forgot to bring these important papers to work." Try to change your language/thinking to be specific and nonjudgmental and stick to the facts of the situation (this can also be very helpful when we are upset with someone). For example, notice the difference between "he never puts things away that I ask and he never cares how I'm feeling," versus "I'm really upset that he didn't put the dishes away today when I asked; when he doesn't do what I ask it makes me feel as if he doesn't care."

> *Example:* Caleb chose to work with the thoughts that he had written the previous day (see above). What struck him when he rewrote these thoughts was that he felt like they were a little more manageable to handle and that he could cope with these situations better. Also, when he adjusted his thinking to become more accurate, he saw some possible coping strategies that had not occurred to him when his thinking was more extreme. Here are his rewritten thoughts:
>
> The traffic might be heavy today as it usually is on Mondays. I know I tend to get tense when I have a longer than usual commute. I have a lot of things scheduled today and that feels a bit overwhelming, though I usually get it all done somehow. (After rewriting this, what occurred to him was that he could bring a podcast to listen to on the way to work to ease the stress of the commute; he also realized he could schedule a few quick breaks throughout the day so that it didn't feel so "endless" to him).
>
> I'm really upset that my son seems to be having trouble handing in his homework. This has happened more than once—I think this is the third time this month. This clearly needs to be addressed. (After stating his thoughts more realistically, Caleb recognized that it might help to contact his son's teacher and

guidance counselor to see if they could assist his son.)

I'm upset that my wife forgot to bring home what I asked for. I know she has a lot that she is juggling, but I'm disappointed. (After rewriting this, Caleb recognized he was in a better mindset to talk with his wife about his disappointment, rather than attack her in an angry, or blameful way.)

EXERCISE THREE

Working with Worry: Distinguishing Between Productive and Unproductive Thinking

One very common form of negative thinking is worry. Worry can be consuming, and it can take us away from the present moment and make us miss out on the here and now of our lives. It can be helpful to become more skilled at distinguishing between the aspects of our negative thinking/worrying that can be turned into productive thought, and those aspects that are unproductive, and can be let go, or moved to the background. Another way to think about this is to ask the following questions:

– What do and don't I have control over in this situation?
– Is there some aspect of this situation that I can do something about right now?
– Can I correct any distorted thinking to make this situation more realistic to cope with?
– What in this situation do I need to accept?

For today's exercise, identify something you are worried about that you find yourself thinking about with some frequency. You could call something up, or notice what arises as you go through your day. You could also choose a worry that has troubled you in the past, if there is nothing current. When you recognize the negative worry thought, stop and ask yourself the above questions. Choose to focus your thinking on what you can control (even if it is just a small aspect of the situation), and see if you can identify any helpful action or steps that you might take. See if you can acknowledge any unproductive thoughts and gently let those go (as you practiced above), or imagine putting those thoughts in the background. If there is an aspect of the situation that you need to accept, see if you can acknowledge this as well and send yourself compassion (e.g., "this is hard"; "this is challenging for me").

Example: Tina chose to work with her worries around the new work project she had been assigned (mentioned earlier in this chapter), which she thought was "awful" and she couldn't imagine completing on time. She recognized her distorted and exaggerated thinking and tried to make it more accurate. She realized that the project wasn't really "awful," but that she felt overwhelmed because there were so many tasks at work that she was being asked to accomplish.

Tina reminded herself that she often felt like this starting new projects, but in the two years she has been at this job, she has never had trouble completing a project or producing good work. She recognized that she had control over a fair amount of this situation (e.g., how she budgeted her time, how efficiently she worked) but that it was still possible it might be challenging for her to finish everything in the time constraints given. Rather than just spinning around negative thoughts in her head and becoming overwhelmed, she realized that she could take certain action steps such as meeting with her boss to express her concerns and see if they might come up with a plan. Also, she could ask some of her coworkers with more experience for help and strategies that might save her some time on the project. She recognized that she needed to accept that she might need to put in some extra work, but also that she could only do what was within reason.

EXERCISE FOUR

Changing Have To's to Get To's

Today is a simple, but enlightening exercise, introduced to me by a colleague, about perspective, and how we choose to look at things. (I have since come across discussions of this by others, who have written about the power of changing these few words (Clear, 2013; Hyatt, 2016; Koch, 2014). It is common as people begin to pay attention to their negative thoughts to notice many thoughts arise involving "have to's" (e.g., I have to go to work today, I have to go grocery shopping, I have to drive my kids all over this afternoon). Usually, these thoughts are experienced in a negative way and involve activities we do not particularly look forward to "having to do." There is often a feeling of stress associated with the "have to" language.

Today, practice turning anything you "have" to do into something that you "get" to do. You can begin, if you like, by writing down all of the things that you "have to" do.

Now take a few minutes and visualize going through your day saying to yourself "get to" instead of "have to." As you actually go through your day, think to yourself about how you "get to" do each of the things you are doing.

Notice what shifts in you when you say to yourself, for example, "I get to go to work today," or "I get to go grocery shopping." Notice how this feels in your body, and how it affects the way you approach the task at hand. Write down what you observe.

> *Example:* Betsy, a busy mother of three children, and a part-time physician, could easily relate to the tendency to think about "have to's" in her life. She found herself trying to fit in so much within a day that she often felt stretched thin. Some of the have to's for her day included driving her kids to school, going to work, buying and cooking food, and helping her children with homework. As she made her "have to" list she felt overwhelmed and stressed anticipating everything she had to do. When she switched this around to "get to," she experienced a noticeable shift in her energy, with a feeling of greater lightness, and gratitude. As she went about her day, she found that she was less irritable and snappy with her children, and she took time to savor and appreciate the 10 minutes that she had with them on the way to school. At work, she found that her thinking focused more than usual on how fortunate she felt that she could help her sick patients, and how grateful she felt to be employed. She approached grocery shopping with a sense of gratitude as well, instead of drudgery, reflecting on how lucky that she could go to a store and buy all the food she needed to feed her family.

EXERCISE FIVE

Changing Radio Stations

As we have discussed previously, there are multiple ways to interpret a situation, and an almost infinite number of things that we can focus our attention on in any given moment. Where we put our attention and our thoughts matters.

Today is an opportunity to practice where you choose to focus your attention and thinking. Take a moment at the beginning of the day to set an intention for yourself:

As you go through your day today, you will make a conscious choice about what "radio station" you listen to in your head; what you "tune into" throughout the day. When you find yourself drifting to negative thoughts, tell yourself to choose another station to dial into. Redirect your attention to something else more helpful to focus on. Let the original negative thoughts drift into the background, so that they become only "background noise" as you choose something different in the foreground. Listen to what the thoughts are on that new radio station. Notice what effect this has on your mood. Notice, too, if you are inclined to behave any differently.

Record your observations.

Example: Ted noticed that much of his energy was drained by thinking frequently about how unreasonable his brother's expectations were, and how no matter what Ted did, he could never seem to do enough in his brother's eyes. These thoughts took a toll on his well-being. So Ted decided that for this exercise, whenever he realized that those thoughts were arising (and this happened fairly frequently because he and his brother worked together at the same family company), he would change the radio station.

The first time he did this, he was sitting by himself at his desk. He took a minute to focus on all the aspects of his job that he really enjoyed as well as all the qualities that he valued in himself at this job. He noticed a definite shift in his mood and energy level. Later, after a challenging interaction with his brother, Ted found himself falling back into these thoughts, especially thoughts about

---

"I'm not enough." He chose to focus his thinking instead on some of the difficult circumstances that shaped his brother's life. He found himself experiencing a bit more compassion for his brother and not taking his behaviors quite so "to heart."

When the thoughts arose a third time, he was thinking about how he resented having to be in this family business with his brother. He shifted his thinking to focus on how grateful he is to be able to do something he is good at and provide a stable income for his family. This allowed him to feel a bit more light-hearted, and he approached the tasks in front of him with more concentration. He found himself joking and smiling more with others.

EXERCISE SIX

Flipping the Switch on Rumination – the Un-Distraction Technique

When you are caught in a particularly strong pull of negative thinking or worry that seems to keep spiraling or is keeping you stuck despite trying the above strategies, this is a good tool to have in your toolkit. Chances are, you already do this to some extent.

As discussed previously, many people say that they will do things to "distract" themselves from their ruminations, such as going for a walk, or doing a crossword puzzle, or playing with their children. Here is an opportunity to begin to think about this differently. The distraction is NOT going for a walk, it is the irrational thoughts which keep spinning needlessly. The walk is choosing to bring one's attention to the present moment, to something here and now, instead of some future thought of "what if" that does not even exist in the real world.

So for this exercise, begin by writing out a list of activities that you can engage in mindfully when you are feeling pulled into a negative cycle of ruminations. It could be something pleasurable (which often works best), but it could also involve a more neutral task, such as cleaning, as long as it is something that can fully engage your attention. (Try to avoid such activities as watching TV or surfing the web).

If you have something on your mind that is distracting and consuming, take some time now to engage in this activity in a mindful way. Bring your awareness fully to the activity, and as those pesky, distracting thoughts arise, practice gently letting them go into the background as you bring your attention back to what you are doing. See if you can allow yourself to bring all of your senses into the activity at hand to help bring you into this moment. If there are no strong negative thoughts you are experiencing now, take a moment and remember a time when you were caught in the pull of ruminations, and use your imagination to rehearse this exercise in your mind. See yourself engaging mindfully in an activity to loosen the grip of your ruminating thoughts.

Example: Roger found that this exercise was perfect timing for him. He had just taken a bad fall yesterday and injured his foot. He was going to the doctor later that day to follow up and see how long his recovery might be, and whether he needed surgery. He found himself being pulled in by ruminating worries as his mind kept thinking about the tennis season around the corner, and several big tournaments he was looking forward to playing in, as he was a serious competitor. The thoughts kept repeating over and over ("Am I going to be able to play this season?" "What if I can't play—what will I do? What if I need surgery?"). Roger chose to go into his basement wood shop to work on a small piece of furniture he was building. Roger used his mindfulness skills to bring his attention over and over to what he was doing—noticing the feel of the saw, the smell of the wood, the sounds of the tools. He found that the thoughts continued to come, but he could put them way off in the background as he became engrossed in what he was doing. When he stopped this activity he found that he was feeling less anxious, and able to look at things with a more accepting perspective.

   EXERCISE SEVEN

Visualization – Feeding Yourself a Healthy Diet of Thoughts

Take a moment to reflect on all the worksheets you filled out this week, what you learned about your own tendency for negative thinking, and what traps you most often fall into. Now set aside five to 10 minutes for the following exercise (use the audio if you like).

Begin by finding a comfortable seated position with your feet on the floor and your spine upright. Take some slow, deep breaths and bring your awareness to your breathing. Follow your breathing for a few cycles, noticing each inhalation and each exhalation. Notice what sensations are present in your body.

When you are ready, take a moment to think about some of the qualities that were most important to you from Week Two. How do you most want to show up in your life?

Now begin to think about the kind of thoughts such a person with these qualities would use to nourish themselves each day. Think about the kind of thoughts you would like to fill your day with, thoughts that are in line with the person you most want to be. Also imagine how you would like to catch yourself as negative thinking creeps in, before it spirals, and what tools would best help you shift away from that negative thinking. Imagine having moments throughout your day where you start to catch yourself in a negative thought stream. Envision yourself using the tools you have been practicing to keep from getting pulled into those negative thoughts. Perhaps you imagine just letting the negative thoughts pass by; perhaps you correct any distorted thinking; perhaps you change a "have to" to a "get to," or imagine changing the radio station and putting the focus of your attention on a more positive, helpful thought.

Notice how this kind of shift feels in your body. Really take a moment to let this feeling sink in, this feeling of not being pulled into negative thoughts, of being able to change the radio station. Perhaps you notice feeling more relaxed, calm, or empowered. Perhaps you notice a lightness in your body. Notice the accompanying emotions as well. Is there room for more joy or gratitude? Notice what changes in your behavior when you are not caught up in taking your negative thinking so seriously. When you are ready, bring your awareness back into the room.

Now, as you go through your day today, notice whether you are able to experience some of what you have envisioned. Make note of any observations on your worksheet and record which skills you were able to incorporate into your day.

WRITING ACTIVITY

FACING CHALLENGES

I was very intrigued to learn that the Chinese word for crisis is made up of two characters, one means "danger," and the other means "opportunity." Take a moment to think about a challenge in your life, something that feels difficult. It could be something current, or something that happened in the past. Set aside a few minutes or more and write about how this situation might be an opportunity in some way. Can you allow yourself to see another side of the situation that perhaps had not occurred to you before?

Example: Roger used this exercise to explore what felt like a current crisis for him: his injured foot, inability to play tennis, and need to have surgery. As he reflected on this situation, he realized it was an opportunity for him to slow down and spend more time in other areas of his life that he had neglected, because tennis took up so much of his time. He realized he could reconnect with a group of friends with whom he had not kept in close touch. In addition, he thought about his passion for photography and how he always put photography classes on the back burner because he did not have enough time to pursue them. He was able to see the opportunity he now had to pursue some of these things.

WEEKLY REFLECTION

- I remind myself today to feed myself with healthy, realistic, accurate, and helpful thoughts to help grow a deeper sense of well-being in my life.

- I recognize that thoughts are just creations in my mind, and do not exist in the world in a concrete way. I choose to take my negative thoughts lightly, and to let them go without sweeping me away with them.

- I recognize that when my thinking is more realistic and accurate, I can cope more easily with the challenges I face.

- I recognize that I have a choice in how I perceive situations. I choose to put the focus of my attention on seeing things from a positive perspective.

♦ As I learn to recognize negative thoughts as they arise, I empower myself to make a different choice and not get swept away by my thoughts in old, habitual ways.

KEY SUMMARY POINTS

• Most of us feed ourselves a daily diet of negative thoughts much more than we realize.

• Often, these negative thoughts can be distorted, inaccurate, unrealistic, and/or exaggerated in some way.

• Our thoughts, interpretations, and perceptions are not fixed; they can be changed, but we need to be aware of what they are in order to change them or choose for them not to have such a hold on us.

• Three basic ways to address our negative thoughts and prevent them from spiraling are:

– Choose to let the negative thought drift into the background by imagining it floating by on a cloud (or some other image) that allows you to recognize this is just a thought created in your mind and not something on which you need to lock your attention.

– Choose to change the thought by correcting any unrealistic thinking and making the thought more accurate and realistic.

– Choose to shift the focus of your attention away from thoughts that are not helpful to ones that are more helpful, and to things going on in this moment that you can be present to.

Week 4, Exercise 1
CATCHING YOUR NEGATIVE THOUGHTS, BIG AND SMALL

Negative Thoughts (note if your thoughts are distorted or irrational)

Physical Sensations

Emotions

Experience of observing your thoughts

Week 4, Exercise 2 **WORKING WITH IRRATIONAL THOUGHTS**	
Write out your negative thoughts:	
Answer the following questions:	Am I making something bigger or worse than it actually is?
	Am I jumping to conclusions about something without evidence to support it?
	Am I thinking in extremes, and is there perhaps a more accurate middle ground?
	Am I predicting or forecasting into the future?
	What evidence do I have that this is a true statement?
	Am I fundamentally doing all right in this moment, right here and now?
Rewrite your negative thoughts, making them more accurate, realistic or true, if appropriate:	

©2017 Beth Kurland, Ph.D.

Week 4, Exercise 3 **WORKING WITH WORRY: DISTINGUISHING BETWEEN PRODUCTIVE AND UNPRODUCTIVE THINKING**	
Name your worries:	
Ask yourself these questions:	What do and don't I have control over in this situation?
	Is there some aspect of this situation that I can do something about right now?
	Can I correct any distorted thinking to make this situation more realistic to cope with?
	What in this situation do I need to accept?
Write down any helpful actions you might take:	
Write down any aspects of the situation you might accept or let go of:	

©2017 Beth Kurland, Ph.D.

Week 4, Exercise 4
CHANGING HAVE TO'S TO GET TO'S

List your "have to's" for today.

Now re-write them as "get to's"

What do you observe in your day, making this shift in your thinking? How does it feel in your body to shift your thinking in this way? How does it affect how you approach the tasks at hand?

Week 4, Exercise 5

CHANGING RADIO STATIONS

Old radio station thoughts:

New radio station thoughts:

Observations: (What is the effect on your mood? What is the effect on your behavior?)

©2017 Beth Kurland, Ph.D.

Week 4, Exercise 6
FLIPPING THE SWITCH ON RUMINATION — THE UN-DISTRACTION TECHNIQUE

Activities to engage in mindfully when ruminations take hold:

Observations after practicing this technique:

©2017 Beth Kurland, Ph.D.

Week 4, Exercise 7

🔊 VISUALIZATION — FEEDING YOURSELF A HEALTHY DIET OF THOUGHTS

Review all of the worksheets from Week 4.

Write down any observations from the visualization exercise:

Make note of any skills you were able to use during your day today:

©2017 Beth Kurland, Ph.D.

Week 4, Writing Activity
FACING CHALLENGES

Write about a challenge in your life:

How might this situation present an opportunity for you in some way?

©2017 Beth Kurland, Ph.D.

WEEK FIVE

EMOTIONAL REGULATION SKILLS

Learning To Embrace Difficult Emotions & Not Get Swept Away

"I tend to be high strung and fly off the handle easily. Having tools to let these feelings arise and notice them without being flooded by them has been immensely helpful. My family has noticed a positive shift in the way I react to things at home." —BERNIE

IN WEEK FOUR, you learned how to recognize the daily diet of unhealthy thoughts you might be feeding yourself, and you learned a number of skills to prevent yourself from getting swept away by negative irrational thoughts and worries. Our emotions also can pull us away from the present moment and spiral us downward if we let them. Learning how to accept and live with difficult emotions is the next step on your journey.

GOALS AND INTENTIONS FOR THIS WEEK

This week, you will learn how to recognize difficult emotions as they arise. You will learn how to be present with these emotions rather than avoid them or push them away. You will also learn ways to stop intense emotions from overtaking you and sweeping you away.

Why Is This Important?

Many of us have learned, directly or indirectly, to push our difficult emotions away when they surface. Some of this is cultural or learned behavior: You may have been told at a young age to "stop crying and pull yourself together"; or to "cut it out and go to your room" when you were upset; or "big kids don't cry," or some other similar message. This tendency to avoid uncomfortable feelings is also human nature; there is a natural tendency to seek pleasure and avoid pain. This is true not just for physical pain, but for emotional pain as well (which, by the way, can be experienced quite physically). It doesn't "feel good" to experience painful emotions, so we often avoid them, thinking this is a good thing for us.

The Cost of Suppressing Emotions

It turns out that avoiding our emotions can often do us more harm than good. Stuffing our feelings deep inside is a bit like putting a lid on a pot of boiling water. After a while, the pressure builds up and if it doesn't have a way to be released, the water can spill over, causing a mess. When we don't pay attention to our emotions, and push them away, they don't actually disappear. They just find some other way to come out. Take a moment to think about a time you may have tried to ignore or push feelings away. It may work for a short while, but usually the emotions end up reappearing with strong force in some way, such as in the form of a meltdown, an anger outburst, or perhaps as anxiety, depression, or physical illness.

The field of Acceptance and Commitment Therapy emphasizes that one of the biggest roadblocks we have to living a valued life is "experiential avoidance," that is, doing everything we can to avoid feeling painful or uncomfortable emotions (Hayes & Smith, 2005). When we run up against uncomfortable feelings (stress, sadness, anxiety, pain), we often do everything in our power to get away from them, or to get rid of them.

This often takes the form of unhelpful behaviors. Sometimes we numb out by unhealthy eating, alcohol, other addictive behaviors, or we lash out in anger, or isolate ourselves and avoid going places where we might feel uncomfortable—to try to avoid experiencing our discomfort. (We explored a little of this in Week Two). When we do this, we often miss out on important parts of our lives and prevent ourselves from embracing the qualities that are most important to us, and doing the things that matter most.

Emotional Hijacking

When we are not avoiding our emotions in some form, many of us can experience being "hijacked" by our emotions, as they take over and spiral us out of control. Daniel Goleman coined this term "emotional hijacking" in his book, *Emotional Intelligence* (1995), to refer to the process by which the more primitive and emotional part of our brain can take over and bypass communication to the higher "thinking" parts of our brain. We have all probably experienced this in some form, perhaps when caught up in a moment of road rage, an argument, being stuck in traffic, being panicked or worried about something, or other situations where we are overtaken by the intensity of our emotions. When that occurs, it is difficult to think clearly, and often, reason and perspective go out the door. This loss of reason and perspective, in combination with the intensity of our emotions, can cause us to react in ways we later regret. There is a good explanation for this from a physiological perspective, and it is helpful to understand what is happening in our brains, so that we can understand what we are trying to "rewire."

Here is a simplified explanation. As we go about our day we receive continual messages from the environment that get processed by a part of our brain called the thalamus. The thalamus sorts out these messages and sends them to both the limbic system, which is the emotional center of our brains, and to the cortex and neocortex, which are the higher thinking parts of our brains. The limbic system is constantly evaluating for perceived danger, through a small organ called the amygdala, and also through the help of the hippocampus. When information is interpreted as emotionally charged by the amygdala, it goes directly to the body's alarm system responsible for turning on the "fight-or-flight" reaction, and to the brainstem, and, in essence bypasses the neocortex (which receives the information only after the alarm system is triggered). Thus, the "fight-or-flight response" gets turned on and we prepare to handle this "emergency" before us (Goleman, 1995). Remember, the limbic system responds not only to life-threatening danger, but also to anything it *perceives* as danger (which could be a conversation that puts us on the defensive, a traffic jam that is preventing us from traveling where we need to be, a look from another person that we believe means they are thinking badly of us, etc.). This system works wonders in a true life-threatening emergency, when we don't have the luxury of that split second that it takes the higher thinking part of our brain, the cortex, to process what is happening. If a car is coming at us, we simply jump out of the way. That extra split second that it would have taken us to discern the speed of the oncoming car and evaluate the situation more accurately could have cost us our life. However, that same split second that it takes for information to get to our cortex might be especially helpful when we are in an argument with someone. It could help us stop and evaluate the situation before becoming emotionally hijacked and blurting out something we later regret.

Learning to Befriend Difficult Emotions

So you may be able to appreciate now that being able to stop and pause when we are overwhelmed by intense emotions can be immensely helpful. It can mean the difference between getting swept away by that emotion entirely, and bringing the cortex "on line" to help put things in perspective and choose how we want to react. When we learn to be present with difficult emotions we create that pause, or "moment of hesitation" (as my brother calls it), to sit and be with what is there. I often like to share this quote by Viktor Frankl, an Austrian psychologist, with my patients: "Between stimulus and response, there is a space. In that space is our power to choose our response. In our response lies our growth and freedom." By taking a moment to stop, breathe, *feel* and *be with* our emotions, we can help create that powerful space.

Learning to stop and be with intense emotions as they arise also prevents us from resorting to our more habitual response (for many of us) of avoiding feelings that are uncomfortable, or pushing them away. When we learn to be with our emotions as they arise we allow them to go through their natural life cycle and move through us, without getting stuck or having to come out in other ways. In addition, as Miriam Greenspan (2003) describes, when we have the courage to be present with "dark" emotions such as fear, despair, and grief, we can experience a kind of alchemy and transformation that allows us to also feel gratitude, faith, and joy.

As you will get to experience shortly, mindfulness skills are essential in our toolkit for emotional regulation. As Ronald Siegel explains so well in his book, *The Mindfulness*

Solution (2010), the more we can increase our capacity to bear uncomfortable emotions, and to be present with whatever is in our direct experience, the more ease we can go through life with, and the less suffering we experience. So to emphasize, the goal is NOT to make difficult feelings go away. It is our goal to try and increase our capacity to experience and bear intense emotions, without being swept away by them.

When I practice this with my patients, we focus on learning to be present with difficult emotions by imagining that we welcome the feelings in, befriend them, allow them to be just as they are. This is often quite the opposite of people's initial inclination, which is to turn away from these feelings. While at first this may seem quite difficult, most people are surprised that it is a relief not to put so much energy into making the feelings go away. They realize that by befriending and turning their attention toward their difficult emotions they are NOT swallowed up by them; in fact, they often experience some sense of ease. I like to use the scene from the movie *The Wizard of Oz*, when Dorothy meets the "great and terrible Oz" to illustrate a point. All along, the wizard has been built up to be some scary, giant monster. When toward the end of the movie the curtain is pulled back, Dorothy discovers that, in fact, the wizard is just a small, meek, ordinary man. So it often is with our feelings. We go to great lengths to avoid our anger, sadness, and fears. However, when we actually allow ourselves to be present to those emotions, we are surprised to realize that we can handle them and bear them. They are no longer so scary to us.

I encourage people to think about sitting with their difficult emotions in the same way you might sit and listen to a good friend—with compassion and non-judgment—and in a space where you are receptive to truly listen (not to berate, advise, invalidate, or otherwise tell the person not to feel what they are feeling). In fact, think for a moment about a time when you shared intense emotions with a good friend who was able to simply listen openly to you. Chances are, having this accepting space to share your emotions was quite helpful, and enabled you to feel calmer. This is what it is like when we can sit mindfully with our feelings. For some people, imagining a parent sitting lovingly with a small child who is feeling sad, anxious, or angry can be a helpful image to bring to mind when sitting with our feelings. We are similar to that loving, accepting parent, and our feelings are like the small child, who simply needs to be accepted, held, and heard.

In the previous week, we focused on noticing our negative thoughts and how they can pull us into a downward spiral. Now we are going to practice some skills that help us manage challenging emotions. Because emotions can become quite intense, and at times overwhelming, it is helpful to have some ways to create a feeling of safety, security, and stability in our bodies, from which we can observe our emotions. The first two exercises will offer that. Please note, if you are currently experiencing very intense emotions (e.g., from a loss or trauma), it may be important to do these exercises with a therapist, or choose less intense emotions with which to practice.

EXERCISE ONE

Dropping Your Anchor

You will need to set aside 5–10 minutes for the initial part of this exercise. Follow along with the audio if you like. Get into a comfortable seated position during a time when there are no distractions around you.

Allow your awareness to turn to your breathing, and begin to follow your breath as it comes in, and as it goes out. Allow your shoulders to drop, allow your face to relax, as you follow your breath in and out.

As you follow your breathing, begin to imagine a ship in the middle of the ocean, and see a big, strong anchor that goes from the ship, down into the water, and deep into the ocean floor. This anchor keeps the ship safe and secure, no matter what the ocean waters are like above. Imagine your breath as a kind of anchor; as you exhale slowly, drop your anchor and see it take hold on the floor beneath you.

Continue to follow your breathing as it comes in and as it goes out. As thoughts arise in your mind, allow them to pass by as you bring your awareness back to your breathing. Imagine for a moment that the waters are calm above you. Take a moment to see if you can find that place of calmness within your own body. See if you can locate a feeling of safety and security inside yourself. You might even recall a time when you felt very safe and secure. Think about that time and notice what happens in your body as you do. You might also imagine going to a familiar place where you feel peaceful, calm, and safe; for example, at the beach.

If you can't feel this inner stability or safety, that's OK. Do not force it. Just hold open the possibility for it as you continue focusing on your breathing and visualize the anchor of the ship. When you are ready, change the scene slightly to one of rough waters at the surface of the ocean. See if you can use your breathing to find your own inner anchor, that sense of calmness that lies beneath the waters if you go deep enough. See if you can imagine the waters rough at the surface, but calm deep underneath. Continue to hold an image of an anchor in your mind, and the sense of stability the anchor represents.

Now imagine that there is a storm at sea. Visualize the storm in all its intensity, and then see the storm passing, as the ship remains safe because it is anchored securely to the ocean floor. As you imagine the storm, see if you can find your "center," that calm, stable place within, and again notice what it feels like in your body. Use your breath to anchor you by returning again and again to your inhalation and exhalation.

Now, when you feel ready, call up a difficult emotion that you are currently experiencing or one that you experienced recently. Choose something that is not too intense or overwhelming: perhaps a recent frustration or irritation, disappointment or stress. See if you can allow this feeling to be present while you continue to focus on your breathing.

Visualize your breath as an anchor, and simply be with whatever feeling is there without needing to change it or make it go away. Stay with this for several minutes, simply being present to whatever feelings arise.

Bring your awareness back into the room when you are ready.

As you go through your day today, notice the emotions that arise and see if you can name them. Several times throughout the day, stop and imagine dropping your anchor and bringing your awareness to your breathing for about a minute or so. Notice what you experience in your body when you do that.

Example: Bernie considers himself a "high strung" person and often feels tense and somewhat anxious. He initially resisted the idea of this exercise, but once he tried it he discovered that it really helped him to feel an internal calmness that he rarely experiences in his day. He liked the idea of allowing the storm to pass while seeing the ship securely anchored in the water. He recognized how easy it is for his own ship to get swept away in the storms when he gets upset. He called up a feeling of irritation that he felt over a recent argument he had with his spouse. Bernie practiced staying "anchored" as he allowed the irritation to be there, and found it helpful to be able to practice not being swept away by his irritation. During his day he noticed irritation, anxiety, worry, anger, and frustration arise. Because he was more aware, he caught the feelings earlier on, before they built up to full intensity. He found it helpful to take a minute several times throughout the day to drop his anchor, and was surprised by the way he could call up that feeling of stability in his body, even during these brief pauses.

EXERCISE TWO

Tree with Roots

Similar to the previous exercise, this exercise will help you create a feeling of safety and stability in your body to help you weather passing emotional storms. The imagery is different, and it can be helpful to try different images and find what works best for you. In this exercise, you will begin as above, finding a comfortable seated position, and turning your awareness to your breathing. An audio of this exercise is available to follow along.

Allow your attention to come back again and again to your breathing, even as emotions or thoughts may try to pull you away. As you inhale, follow the inhalation all the way up through your body, and as you exhale follow the exhalation all the way from your head to your feet. Do this for several minutes.

Now turn your awareness to the bottoms of your feet. Feel the souls of your feet making contact with the ground beneath you. Notice any sensations in the bottoms of your feet, as you feel them supported by the ground.

Now imagine that tree roots extend from the soles of your feet down deep into the earth beneath you, and spread out far and wide. See these roots growing deep into the ground, and visualize them as strong and solid.

Next, imagine a beautiful, healthy tree above the ground that is connected to the earth with these roots; the roots provide stability, security, and nourishment for the tree.

As you breathe in, imagine drawing up nourishment from the earth, through the roots, into the trunk and branches of the tree. Stay with this focus on your inhalation for several cycles of breath.

When you are ready, imagine a radiant, golden sun above your head shining down on the tree and all its leaves and branches. As you take in the sunlight and its nourishment and warmth, focus on your exhalation and follow it all the way down to the soles of your feet.

After a few cycles of focusing on your exhalation, you can alternate focusing on both the inhalation and exhalation, drawing up nourishment from the roots as you inhale, and bringing replenishing light down through the body of the tree, and your own body, as you breathe out. Take a moment to sense into your body, and notice any feelings of safety, stability, and being grounded. Allow these feelings to grow inside of you.

When you are ready, imagine that the weather begins to change, and see strong winds blowing the tree and its branches and leaves. As you watch the winds pick up, notice that the tree is safely rooted in the ground. Now imagine storms—perhaps rain, thunder, snow—and see that through all kinds of weather, the tree remains securely rooted. Watch the storms pass, and see the sun returning.

Now think about your day ahead. Note that there may be passing emotional storms. Imagine yourself weathering these storms, finding that inner sense of security even amid intense emotions that may come up throughout the day. Envision yourself remembering and calling up that feeling of being rooted and stable as challenging emotions arise during the day.

Notice how your body feels when you can access your own roots and sense of stability. Watch the storms pass you without being swept away by them. When you are ready, come back into the room.

> *Example*: Gina initially found this exercise challenging because her mind was running in so many different directions, but she stayed with it. At first she felt angry at herself for not being more focused, but then she caught herself judging herself. She was then able to imagine her passing thoughts like the wind blowing through the branches, and this helped her mind to settle down. She realized she

couldn't stop her thoughts any more than she could stop the wind. Gina saw this as an opportunity to practice being with her anger and irritation at herself, (which were familiar feelings for her since she was a perfectionist and often hard on herself). Gina found the image of the tree and roots very calming to her body, and she liked the sensation of her feet grounded on the floor. She envisioned that when she started to get frustrated with her children, she could stop and feel her feet and imagine the tree roots, and a feeling of safety in her own body, before reacting to her children.

EXERCISE THREE

The Hurricane Exercise – Catching Difficult Emotions

Today you will have the opportunity to try your hand at meteorology. Your job is to observe your emotions closely throughout the day as if you were a meteorologist observing a hurricane. Your job is not to make any predictions, but simply to notice, label, and narrate to yourself what you see.

When you are aware of a challenging emotion arising, name it (e.g., frustration, anger, rage, sadness) and then decide how intense it is using a 1–5 scale—similar to rating a hurricane category 1 through 5 (category 1 being mild and category 5 being the most out of control and intense). As you notice challenging feelings in your body, see if you can call up the image of the ship and its anchor, or the tree with roots, while you are experiencing the feelings.

Be aware of yourself as separate from your feelings, reminding yourself that you are not your feelings; they are simply a transient experience within you. Like the hurricane or storm, they will pass.

Take some time to write down your observations on your worksheet.

Example: Petra's most challenging moment of the day was in the morning when her daughter had a meltdown after she was unable to find any clothes that she wanted to wear. At the same time, Petra needed to get her and her daughter out the door on time so she would not be late for work. She noted that she was feeling intensely frustrated, and rated this as a category three storm. She started to fly off the handle and have her own meltdown in reaction to her daughter's behavior. She remembered the exercise and shut herself in the bathroom for a moment and visualized a huge storm at sea. She took several conscious breaths and imagined dropping her anchor so as not to be completely swept away. This helped to prevent the hurricane from being upgraded to a category four storm. As she was able to experience a momentary calm within the storm (like being in the eye of a hurricane, she imagined), she was able to think clearly enough to realize that her own huge reaction would just make things worse, and she was able to keep her behavior in check.

EXERCISE FOUR

Being with Frustration

Today you will have an opportunity to practice being with your own frustration, by making direct contact with it through this mindfulness exercise. Set aside some time when you will not be interrupted for at least 5–10 minutes. You may follow along with the guided audio if you like.

Think about something that makes you feel frustrated (though make sure it is not something traumatic, or something that would bring up overwhelming emotions for you). It could be something that happened recently, such as an argument, or perhaps something that happened on the day you did the previous exercise, or any situation that allows you to call up feelings of frustration. (If you prefer and it feels more relevant at the moment, you could instead focus on a feeling, such as disappointment or irritation).

Rather than turning away from those feelings, take the next few minutes to turn toward those feelings. Imagine doing this by inviting your frustration into the room and seeing yourself observing your frustration in a compassionate way. You might imagine your frustration as a color, or perhaps even as a human figure, cartoon figure, or child.

Notice what it is like to allow the frustration to be there and allow yourself to be present to it. Pay attention to how your body feels.

- Is there tension?
- Do you want to push it away?
- Is there any part of you that softens as you sit with your frustration?

Notice what happens to the frustration as you turn your attention toward it. See if you can call up feelings of compassion towards yourself and allow those feelings to surround you as you sit with the frustration. You can use your breath to help create an anchor for yourself, or bring awareness to your feet and envision roots going into the ground, to help keep you from being pulled away by your feelings. As you sit with it, notice what if anything changes.

When this exercise feels complete, take a moment to write down your observations on your worksheet.

Example: Petra used this exercise as a chance to sit further with the frustration that arose the day before when her daughter was having a meltdown. She was able to call up that experience easily, and with it, the feelings of frustration that she felt. She realized that her initial inclination was to make the feelings go away because they were uncomfortable, but she practiced making space for them and allowing them just to be there, without her needing to react to them. She realized that when she feels frustrated like that during a situation, she often resorts to yelling and screaming as a way of trying to make the feelings go away, by forcing the situation to be different than it is. She imagined her frustration as a funny looking cartoon character similar to a troll, stamping and carrying on. She noticed a lot of tension in her body initially, but as she sat with her frustration, observed it and just allowed it to be there, she noticed that this tension began to dissipate. She could even see her frustrated "troll" settle down a bit as she focused her attention on him. She noticed negative thoughts arising that she wasn't a good mother for having her own meltdown, but she tried to let these thoughts go and focus on a feeling of compassion. It was easiest to do this when she thought of all her friends with young children, who struggled with similar parenting challenges. She could feel compassion toward their frustration, so she was then able to direct this back to herself.

Later in the day Petra had a chance to practice this in "real time" when her daughter began to have another meltdown. Having gone through this exercise and practiced being with her frustration without getting swept away by it, she had a sense of how this feels and was able to catch herself earlier, before her emotions intensified to a point of no return. She found it especially helpful to try and call up some compassion for herself by remembering that she was not alone in what she was experiencing; thousands of other parents struggle with similar situations and emotions.

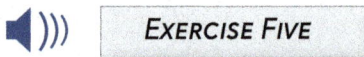

EXERCISE FIVE

Being with Anxiety (and Stepping out of Your Comfort Zone)

Today you will have an opportunity to befriend your anxiety or discomfort in stepping out of your "comfort zone." For the purpose of this exercise, think about something that you would like to do, but haven't done because it has felt uncomfortable in some way, or has created anxiety for you. For example, you might want to share more ideas during work meetings but feel self-conscious; you may want to call someone and ask them on a date but have been putting it off because you are anxious; you may want to have a dinner party but are worried it may not go over perfectly; or, you may want to take a drawing class but feel self-doubt about your artistic talents.

Alternatively, you could think about something that you have been wanting to do that you know would be good for you (eating healthier, organizing your house, exercising) but you have been putting off for some reason. In that case, focus on the feeling of resistance or what stops you from doing this thing.

Part One: Once you have something in mind, set aside about 10 minutes for part one of this exercise. Imagine yourself wanting to take a certain action, but notice the feelings that you are avoiding that keep you from doing it. Follow the instructions in Exercise Four (or listen to the accompanying audio), substituting the word "frustration" with "anxiety" or "discomfort." You will be turning your attention toward this uncomfortable feeling that gets in the way of taking action. Pay close attention to the tendency to avoid feeling this discomfort, and see if you can turn toward it and allow it into the room so that you can observe it.

Once you have been present with this emotion for a while, there is an additional part of this exercise. Take a moment to imagine yourself doing that thing that you have been resisting. Rather than needing these uncomfortable feelings to be gone, see if you can imagine taking them along with you, but perhaps putting them in the "back seat" so to speak, or in the background somewhere. These feelings may still be a part of your experience but they don't take over and run the show. You still get to choose what you want to do, while holding a space for these emotions to be there but not stop you. As with the previous exercise, see if you can bring a feeling of compassion to yourself, perhaps by thinking about all the other people in the world who have experienced similar feelings.

Part Two: As you go through the day today, see if you can take a small step toward doing that thing that you want to do (e.g., make that phone call, put that art class on your calendar, speak up at work, start planning the guest list for your party, go to the gym). As you take a step out of your comfort zone, see if you can make a space for those uncomfortable feelings and bring them along with you in the back seat.

Use the worksheet to write down what you did and what you observed about your emotions. If there is no action step that you can take today, write down what step you would like to take and when you will implement it.

Examples: Justin (from Week Two) chose to sit with his anxiety related to his procrastination in organizing his life. He was aware from Week Two that being more organized was something that is important to him, but he put it off because of the anxiety he would have to face dealing with his clutter and mess. Instead of his usual pattern of avoiding, Justin chose to turn toward this anxiety through this exercise. At first as he tried to be present with these feelings, he had the image of a big black cloud above him almost swallowing him up. As he sat with this feeling longer, and tried to observe it, he was able to gain some distance from the cloud and see it as separate from himself. The more he turned his attention toward this image of the cloud and the accompanying feeling in his body, the more comfortable he became with it. It no longer felt quite so big, bad, and terrible.

Justin was able to imagine himself taking a small step and organizing the stacks of papers on his desk. As he imagined this, he pictured his black cloud as a small cloud off to the side, and not directly overhead. He visualized experiencing some anxiety in his body as he approached the task, but he saw it as manageable and did not let it stop him from completing his task. Later, Justin was able to carry out what he had visualized earlier, and felt a great sense of relief for being able to start something he had put off for so long. Taking this small step was an important catalyst for change.

Carol (from Week Two) had identified from earlier exercises that she wanted to take better care of herself, but she was aware of some anxiety getting in the way, especially when she thought about going to a yoga class. She worried about being judged for not being in good shape. She focused on this feeling of anxiety for this exercise, imagining going to the yoga class and noticing the feelings that arose as she called this to mind. She experienced her anxiety as a strong pressure in her chest with a rapid heartbeat, as well as knots in her stomach.

As she stayed with this feeling in her body and tried to bring her attention to it she also had an image of her anxiety as a fearful little girl. She imagined feelings of compassion toward the little girl, the same way that she felt toward her own children when they were scared. She visualized herself going into the yoga class holding the little girl's hand, comforting her, and sitting near her while she enjoyed the class. Carol was not able to go to a yoga class that day due to her schedule, but she did take the step of signing up for one online for Saturday. Having taken that action, she felt more certain that she would carry it out and actually go.

EXERCISE SIX

Practicing the Moment of Hesitation

Today, as you go through your day, you will have the opportunity to practice the "moment of hesitation." Notice what emotions arise throughout the day. Be a careful observer and as you become aware of any challenging emotions arising, take a moment to pause, and be with that feeling. See if you can catch the feelings early, before they intensify too much.

Take several slow, deliberate breaths and bring your awareness to the feeling and how it shows up in your body. Take a moment to bring your breath into any uncomfortable places in your body. Send some compassion to yourself and think about how so many other people experience similar situations and emotions.

You could take as little as 30 seconds to do this, a minute, or more if you like. See if you can use this moment of hesitation before reacting to what you are feeling. Write down on the worksheet what emotions arose throughout the day, and what you noticed when you used the moment of hesitation.

> *Example*: Richard, from Week One, recognized that he tended to fly off the handle at work and react impulsively with his employees when small things went wrong. As he brought mindful awareness to his emotions throughout the day, he was able to catch his irritability and agitation in the earlier stages, when it was easier to keep from being hijacked by his own feelings. As one example, he came across an error by one of his new employees and normally would have reacted immediately. Instead, he took a minute to be with his rising feeling of anger. In that moment, he recalled what it was like when his own father, who was a perfectionist, yelled at him for making mistakes. His tense muscles relaxed slightly as he breathed through his anger. When he went to speak with the employee just after this, his words were well planned and he was able to address the situation at hand more effectively.

EXERCISE SEVEN

Putting It All Together

For this visualization exercise you can follow along with the audio or simply follow the instructions here. Set aside about 10 minutes when you will not be interrupted. Begin by finding a comfortable seated position and bringing your awareness to your breathing.

Spend a few minutes taking slow, deliberate breaths and following your breath as it comes in and goes out. Let the thoughts in your mind pass by as they arise and bring your focus back to your breathing. When you are ready, you can imagine that there is a TV screen in front of you where you can see scenes from your life.

Take a moment to look into the recent past and notice ways that you have not always handled emotions in the most helpful manner. You might see a scene in which you flew off the handle, pushed away emotions such as sadness (that may have needed your attention), let anxiety stop you from doing something that you wanted, reacted by getting swept away by an emotion and later regretted your behavior, or anything else that comes to mind. As you watch this scene, try not to judge yourself, but simply observe some of the challenges you have faced in dealing with your emotions, and know that you are in good company. Acknowledge that you are human, and see if you can bring a feeling of compassion to yourself for this.

As you continue to watch this scene, try to notice the moment when you got pulled in and swept away by your emotions, and imagine that you could freeze-frame this scene and find that split second when you could have used a moment of hesitation.

Now, when you are ready, let that scene go and begin to flash forward into your week ahead. See yourself going through the day and week ahead with an awareness and open acceptance of the emotions that arise throughout your day. See yourself as having a greater capacity to hold a space for your feelings, without reacting automatically.

Imagine different situations in which you might use your breath as an anchor. Imagine your tree with roots, see yourself sitting with a difficult emotion, and using the moment of hesitation to break free from your old, automatic programs. Really take some time to visualize using these tools in situations that might arise throughout your day.

Make sure to notice what you feel in your body as you do this. Is there a growing sense of calmness, a feeling of having more space within, perhaps a feeling of empowerment, or confidence in being able to be present with difficult emotions? Whatever is there, simply notice it, and allow this feeling to grow inside of you. Spend as much time with this exercise as you like.

As you go through your day today, notice in what ways you are able to recreate this new emotional scene that you just envisioned. Notice what tools you are able to use to allow difficult feelings in, and to not be swept away by them.

Make sure to write down what you observe about your day on your worksheet, including what tools are most helpful for you.

WRITING ACTIVITY
THREE BOXES

For this activity, you can use paper and pencil to draw three boxes of different sizes: one large box, one medium box, and one small box. Alternatively you could use three nesting boxes if you like.

In the largest box, write down the emotions that you tend to show to the outside world; in other words, the "face" that most others see. In the medium box, take some time to reflect on the emotional side of yourself that you tend to show only your closest family members and friends; in other words, the emotions that may be under the surface. For the smallest box, reflect on the emotions you tend to push away and don't let anyone else see, perhaps not even yourself.

After going through this exercise, see if there are any small steps that might help to make more space, or bring acceptance or compassion to some of your deeper or more hidden emotions.

> *Example*: Tamika recognized from this exercise that she likes people to see her as funny, upbeat, happy, energetic, and kind—and these are the emotions she tends to show the outside world (which she put into her largest box). For the medium box, Tamika realized that she tended to show only her close family and friends her irritability, frustration, anger and worry. For her smallest box, Tamika put sadness inside. She recognized that this is an emotion she hardly allows herself to experience, let alone let anyone else see. As a child, she was given strong messages from her family that it was not OK to show sadness, so she automatically began to stuff her sadness away. She was aware that the price she paid for this was that emotions built up in her and came out in other ways (such as physical illness, and feeling emotionally drained). Tamika decided that it would help to begin to make some space for her to acknowledge, feel, and be with her sadness as it arose, and that this was not a "bad" or unacceptable feeling. In order to practice this, she decided to set aside some time during the week when she could watch a sad movie and allow herself to feel her sadness rather than push it away or avoid it.

WEEKLY REFLECTION

- I have the ability to access a sense of safety and stability within myself, from which it is easier to allow myself to feel and observe challenging emotions.

- I practice accepting and befriending all of my emotions, even the uncomfortable ones.

- When I embrace all my emotions, I live life more fully, I am more whole, and I can better choose how I behave and react.

- I choose to be more conscious of my emotions as they arise, and I choose to take time to pause mindfully so as not to be swept away by my feelings.

SUMMARY OF KEY POINTS

- As human beings, there is a tendency, when we experience difficult emotions, to either avoid feeling these painful emotions, or to become "emotionally hijacked" by them and swept away.

- Either of these things can have negative consequences for our health and well-being.

- Learning to accept, be with, and even welcome difficult emotions is a skill that can be practiced and learned. Mindfulness offers us a way to do this.

- Learning to be present with our feelings, even the uncomfortable ones, helps us be less reactive and more thoughtful and conscious about how we behave. It can help us stop reacting in ways we later regret, while at the same time help us act in ways we prefer.

- Practicing and using the skills from this chapter can help you befriend your difficult emotions and create a greater sense of well-being and ease.

Week 5, Exercise 1
DROPPING YOUR ANCHOR

Observations during your day:

Situation

Emotion

Able to "drop your anchor" (yes/no)

Observations

©2017 Beth Kurland, Ph.D.

Week 5, Exercise 2
TREE WITH ROOTS

Observations from visualization exercise:

Ways that you might use this in your day or week ahead:

	Week 5, Exercise 3 **THE HURRICANE EXERCISE — CATCHING DIFFICULT EMOTIONS**		
Emotion	Intensity (1–5)	Able to visualize the tree with roots or anchor (yes/no)	Observations
			©2017 Beth Kurland, Ph.D.

Week 5, Exercise 4

🔊)))

BEING WITH FRUSTRATION

Write down any observations from the meditation:

Write about any opportunities to practice being with frustration during your day. What did you observe? Were you able to bring feelings of compassion to yourself?

	Week 5, Exercise 5 🔊)) **BEING WITH ANXIETY** **(and Stepping out of Your Comfort Zone)**
	**Part One**
Name something you would like to do, but haven't, due to discomfort.	
Write down any observations from the meditation exercise:	
	**Part Two**
Small action taken today	
Emotions	
Observations	
Or,	
Action you would like to take:	
By when:	

©2017 Beth Kurland, Ph.D.

	Week 5, Exercise 6		
	PRACTICING THE MOMENT OF HESITATION		
Emotions	Able to pause (yes/no)	Observations	Consequences of Pausing

©2017 Beth Kurland, Ph.D.

Week 5, Exercise 7

PUTTING IT ALL TOGETHER

Observations from meditation:

What tools were you able to use today to help cope with difficult feelings?
Which tools were most helpful?

©2017 Beth Kurland, Ph.D.

Week 5, Writing Activity
THREE BOXES

Emotions you show to the outside world:

Emotions you show only to close family members or friends:

Emotions you tend to push away, or don't let anyone else see:

Name any steps you could take to make more space for, or bring more acceptance or compassion, to your deepest, hidden emotions:

WEEK SIX

CULTIVATING POSITIVE EMOTIONS (PART 1)

How Small Actions Hold the Key to Happiness

"I used to think a lot about just 'getting through my day,' as if it was something to race through and get to the end of. I didn't realize the little things that I was missing along the way that I now have learned to stop and appreciate more." —Pamela

Up until this point, we have focused on learning tools to manage stress and cope with difficult emotions. You have learned how to bring more mindful awareness to your thoughts, feelings and behaviors, especially when stress and negativity creep in and take over. You have also developed a roadmap to guide you each day toward those things you most value in your life. With this as a foundation, it is now time to begin to intentionally create positive experiences in your life.

GOALS AND INTENTIONS FOR THIS WEEK

This week's goal is to learn to cultivate positive emotional experiences through intentional behaviors and actions. Instead of just going through the motions of our day, we can choose to engage in behaviors that will enhance our day and our well-being.

Why Is This Important?

Many of us go through life thinking, *if I only I could* _____ (retire, win the lottery, get that new job, get through this week, get through the winter, move to a new house, pay off my debts, etc.), then I'll be happy. The problem is that when we think this way, we often end up waiting for "someday" and miss out on the "little things"—the day-to-day joys and opportunities that were right in front of us all along.

What Truly Makes Us Happy?

The growing field of Positive Psychology has contributed greatly to research on happiness and to understanding what helps people feel happy. One of the key concepts that has emerged from this research is that happiness is not something that happens to you; it is something that you can create each day through your actions. In her book, *The How of Happiness*, Sonja Lyubomirsky (2008) describes how she and other researchers discovered some surprising answers to the question of what determines happiness. Only about 10% of an individual's happiness is determined by their life circumstances (i.e., both the "good" and the "bad" things that happen in their lifetime). They found that about 50% of happiness is genetically determined, but that a large 40% is determined by intentional activity.

In other words, each of us tends to have a happiness set point, or baseline of happiness determined by our temperament and wiring at birth. When good things and bad things happen in our lives, we may temporarily feel very happy or very unhappy, but over time we tend to return to this "set point." However, to a large extent, this set point can be changed by the kinds of activities in which we engage in, so our behavior can significantly determine our happiness. Lyubomirsky outlines twelve happiness-increasing strategies. Research suggests that engaging in any or all of these can increase a person's happiness. These activities include: expressing gratitude, nurturing relationships, practicing acts of kindness, doing more activities that truly engage you, savoring life's joys, committing to your goals, and taking care of your body (Lyubomirsky, 2008).

Another groundbreaking book by a pioneer in the field of Positive Psychology is *Positivity* by Barbara Fredrickson (2009). Barbara Fredrickson has made a career out of studying positive emotions such as joy, serenity, interest, love, gratitude, and inspiration. She uses the term "positivity" to describe this "secret ingredient" to a happy life and says that we all have this ingredient within us, but most of us don't access it fully. Fredrickson found some ways to increase positivity include: finding positive meaning in difficult situations (we will work more with this in the next chapter), savoring the good, practicing gratitude, practicing acts of kindness, engaging in activities you are passionate about, and visualizing your future success in great detail (Fredrickson, 2009).

The Benefits of Increasing Positivity

According to Dr. Fredrickson, the benefits of increasing positivity in our lives include the following:

1. It feels good, and the more you get of it, the more you want;

2. It changes how your mind works: it broadens the possibilities that your mind can see, allows you to think more creatively and flexibly; allows you to see things that you might not otherwise see;

3. It transforms your future by building resources: it improves your sleep and health; helps you be more mindful; increases optimism and resiliency; and improves connections with others;

4. It puts the breaks on negativity—it's like hitting a reset button;

5. Increasing positivity obeys a "tipping point" that is nonlinear in that once you achieve a certain amount of positivity, small positive changes can lead to huge differences in one's life.

According to Dr. Fredrickson, positivity carries with it an upward momentum that can lead to extraordinary outcomes. The exciting thing about this research is that positivity is something we can increase through our thoughts and actions. Importantly, Dr. Fredrickson points out, positivity is not the result of being healthy or successful. It is what CREATES success and health. People who have more positivity actually live longer, have more successful marriages, and bigger salaries (Fredrickson, 2009).

The Power of Momentum

Barbara Fredrickson's research suggests that if every negative emotional experience is balanced by at least three authentic, heartfelt, positive experiences (in other words, if we can experience a 3:1 ratio of positivity to negativity, or higher), we can reach a critical "tipping point" at which we can transform our lives from just getting by to thriving and flourishing. Living below this ratio, it is easier to be pulled into a downward spiral of negativity, but reaching this ratio or higher helps people become energized, creative, joyful, and uplifted (Fredrickson, 2009).

I can testify that in my own clinical practice, I have repeatedly seen the power in my patients' lives of what I refer to as "momentum." Even people with severe depression, who begin to engage in small, positive daily experiences can transform a downward spiral into an upward spiral, where increasingly they build positive "momentum" that carries them out of their depression to a place of feeling whole again. But you certainly don't need to be clinically depressed to experience the power of positivity's pull. For many, it can be the difference between just getting by, "surviving" in one's day-to-day life, and truly feeling like you are alive and living fully.

The research in Positive Psychology has shown that one important key to cultivating positivity is to commit to daily and weekly actions that help to cultivate these positive emotions. In the exercises that follow, the focus is on helping you engage in specific *behaviors* that will help generate positive emotions. In the following chapter, we will work on cultivating positive emotions by using our minds and our thinking to generate positive feelings.

One important element of these exercises and those that follow in Week Seven, is to notice and savor the positive emotions that are evoked. Neuropsychologist Rick Hanson, in his book, *Hardwiring Happiness* (2013), writes that we can grow inner strength and resilience and rewire our brain to experience the good by a process of having a positive experience, and then enriching it and absorbing it. Hanson describes how the critical step of paying attention to positive emotional experiences, for even a minute or less, over time helps to shape the neural structures in our brains and, in essence, "install" them (Hanson, 2013, p. 28). Several of the exercises to follow are inspired by his work.

EXERCISE ONE

Being in Nature

Today, you will have the opportunity to enjoy a gift that is available to all of us: nature. Becoming mindful of the natural beauty around us and engaging our senses in the presence of nature can bring about positive emotions such as peace, calmness, awe, inspiration, and relaxation. Set aside 10 minutes for today's exercise. If you are able, go outside for this exercise somewhere that allows you to connect with nature. It need not be any further than your own doorstep. Look for a spot where there is grass, a tree, flowers or plants, or even just some fresh air and sunshine. If you are unable to get outside, you can do this exercise using your imagination, by going to a place of natural beauty in your mind, such as a beach or meadow, or by looking at a picture of something or some place in nature.

Once you have selected from one of these options, focus your attention on it (you could focus on a natural object within your surroundings, such as a rock or tree, the setting itself, such as the beach or the woods, or even a sensation, such as the feeling of sunshine on your skin). Take time to be fully present with whatever you are focusing on, by engaging as many of your senses as possible. For example, if you are focusing on a stone you might pick it up and notice its shape and color; you might feel its texture and temperature and weight; you might listen to the sound it makes as it falls to the ground; you might smell its earthy aroma. If you are sitting outside you could take in the sight of the trees around you, feel the breeze against your skin, or be aware of the warmth of the sunshine on your face. See if you can immerse yourself in this experience of being in nature as fully as possible.

If your mind wanders to other things, gently guide it back to your experience of nature, again and again. Take some time to notice what you are feeling as you are doing this activity. What emotions are you experiencing? What sensations are you feeling within your body?

When this exercise is complete for you, take a moment to write down your observations of this experience.

Example: Pamela decided to spend 10 minutes sitting in her back yard in between getting her children off to school and having to go to work. She was aware that this is not usually time she takes for herself, and she appreciated having the 10 quiet minutes where no demands were being made of her. As she sat in her yard she also became aware of how much she looks at her yard, but never really sees it, amidst her hurried life. She found it soothing to watch the colors of the leaves blowing gently in the breeze, and to feel the warmth of the sunshine spreading across her body. She enjoyed listening to the songs of the many birds in her yard, which she also realized that she rarely noticed. In this short time, Pamela experienced tension draining from her body and felt a sense of relaxation and serenity. She found this experience deeply restorative, and it helped to bring positive energy into her day.

EXERCISE TWO

Doing What You Love and Being in Flow

Today you will set aside a minimum of 10 minutes—or a longer period of time if that is possible—to get the full benefit of this exercise. You will be generating positive emotions by choosing an activity that you deeply enjoy and that allows you to be fully absorbed in the experience. Some people refer to this feeling as "being in the flow."

When you are fully immersed in doing something, there is a state of ease, and you may even experience a sense of no time, or time standing still. When we are fully present in an activity like this, there are positive emotions that naturally emerge. For some people, activities such as running, hiking, cooking, knitting, painting, dancing, listening to music, or doing a puzzle might put them into this mode of being present and engaged.

Think about what might work best for you, and see if you can arrange to do that thing today. As you are engaging in this activity, see if you can bring your full awareness to it so that you can fully absorb the experience and the accompanying feelings that it generates.

Take a moment to name the emotions that you are experiencing, and notice what sensations are present in your body. If your mind wanders, see if you can gently guide it back to the activity at hand. Bring your attention to what you are doing and see if you can savor this experience by noticing any positive emotions and allowing those feelings to grow and expand inside you.

> *Example:* Channah was struggling with depression, and working with a therapist who encouraged her to try this exercise. She was finding it very difficult to get out of bed and get up and going during the day. Her body felt heavy and weighted down, she had very little motivation to do anything, and she felt stuck in the pull of negativity. Because Channah loved woodworking and was quite creative in this area, she decided to spend some time doing this. It was something she used to do often, but had abandoned as her depression deepened. While it took great effort to initiate, once Channah began using her tools she remembered how much she enjoyed this. She had intended to spend just 10 or 15 minutes using her tools so she could tell her therapist she had done it, but she found herself quite engaged once she allowed herself to become immersed in what she was doing. What she noticed most during this activity was a feeling of lightness and energy in her body that she hadn't experienced in a long time. She felt less depressed and more peaceful, and this feeling carried with it some positive momentum into her day.

EXERCISE THREE

Gratitude through Action

One very powerful and well-researched way of generating positive emotions is by practicing gratitude. Due to our brain's negativity bias, it can be easier to notice negatives than positives in our lives. Consciously focusing our attention on our reasons to be grateful can help us generate important positive emotions.

Today, you will have the opportunity to experience gratitude and act on that feeling by expressing it to someone else. This is a particularly powerful way to experience the benefits of gratitude, and to have the double benefit of sharing it with someone else.

Think about someone for whom you are grateful in your life, or perhaps something that someone did for which you are grateful. It could be feeling grateful for a partner or friend, parent or child in your life; it could be appreciation toward an employee for their hard work, toward a child for helping you in some way, or even toward a cashier who is friendly, cheerful, or patient. Find an opportunity today to express gratitude to a person of your choosing. Some ways of doing this might include sending a card, email or text to let someone know how much they mean to you, going out of your way to thank someone for their efforts, or in some other way expressing appreciation to someone to whom you would not normally express gratitude.

After you do this, write down on your worksheet what you noticed about this experience and what feelings it generated in you.

> *Examples:* Frank, introduced in Week One, tended to get stressed and upset about his teenage son's behavior. He would often point out things his son wasn't doing, or ask him to do things that needed to be done, but he was much less likely to express his love for his son. He decided to send his son a text, telling him how lucky he was to have him for a son, and how he enjoyed watching his son grow into the person he had become. Taking the few minutes to express these heartfelt emotions called up feelings for Frank of warmth and love, feelings that he found were uplifting and added joy to his day. The impact of his words also helped create a stronger, more positive connection with his son that he was able to continue to work on fostering.
>
> Richard, who was first mentioned in Week One, had a tendency to notice and criticize his employees when they did something wrong, but he realized that he rarely took the time to let them know when they were doing a good job. He decided to take a few minutes during the day to walk around to several employees and let them know how much he appreciated their effort at work. It felt surprisingly good to do this, and he experienced pleasure in seeing the response of his employees, who were not expecting his approval. He noted the positive shift in the energy in his work environment through these simple actions, and this prompted him to make a point of doing this more often.

EXERCISE FOUR

Compassion through Actions

Today you will have an opportunity to generate feelings of compassion through actions that involve doing something loving for someone else. Some examples of this include: surprising a partner with a favorite dinner, paying a visit to an elderly person or new neighbor, bringing flowers to a friend who is going through a difficult time, calling someone by phone who is lonely and would appreciate the call, cuddling with a small child, spending some extra time with a beloved pet, giving a loved one a massage, and delivering food to a food pantry. Find an action that speaks to you and is meaningful. Notice the feelings generated in you when you engage in this action, and take some time to let any positive feelings spread and grow within you.

> *Example:* Karen (from Week Three) was working on reducing her stress by trying to live life less frenetically and at a slower pace. Despite her busy day, she decided to stop and buy some homemade soup from her favorite restaurant to bring to her neighbor, whom she knew had been sick for several days. In her old way of operating, she might have had this idea but would not have acted on it because she was too busy. However, she noticed how good it felt to take the time out of her day to do this small gesture. She noticed that she felt happy and lighthearted as she drove home with the soup, even though she had a lot to do that evening. Rather than focusing on everything she had to do and feeling stressed, she was conscious of enjoying the good feeling of doing something for someone else. She tried to allow herself to savor this good feeling and carry it with her into her evening. She also noticed a feeling of connection in reaching out to her neighbor that made her feel part of something larger than herself, a feeling that enriched her evening and brought a sensation of warmth to her heart.

EXERCISE FIVE

Generating Positive Emotions through Small, Random Displays of Kindness

The previous exercise was an opportunity to engage in a compassionate action by planning it and carrying it out. Today will be a variation on that exercise, and will give you a chance to generate positive emotions a bit more spontaneously. Your task today is to look for any and all opportunities during your day, in which you can share a moment of kindness or positivity through a small gesture or action. Some simple examples of this include: taking a moment to give family members a hello or goodbye hug, looking a cashier in the eyes as you thank them, giving a coworker a warm hello, holding the door open for someone, letting someone go in front of you in line who looks like they are in a hurry, or perhaps even paying for the toll of the car behind you. Look for things you can do within the natural course of your day that don't require much extra time on your part. It might be as simple as changing the tone of your voice when you speak to someone. As you go through your day, notice how these small actions makes you feel inside.

In your workbook, write down everything you did, and how you felt.

> *Example:* Tilak found that this exercise changed his day from ordinary and mundane, to fun and enjoyable. He viewed it as a kind of private challenge or game to try to find opportunities in which he could be kind or positive where he might otherwise be caught up in his own head or his own stress. Rather than rushing out of the house in the morning as usual, he took a moment to give his sons and wife an affectionate hug. At the pharmacy, he smiled and joked briefly with the people waiting in line, before busying himself with his phone as he usually did. At work, he made it a point to make more eye contact with people as he walked past, and to ask coworkers how they were doing. When he paid his toll driving home from work, he paid attention to the tone of his voice and said "hey thanks, have a good day" in a genuinely kind way, and truly meant what he said. Tilak was aware that none of these things took more time in his day, yet they definitely shifted his mood and allowed him to experience more positivity.

EXERCISE SIX

Loving-Kindness toward Oneself

You have had the chance to practice kindness and compassion towards others; now you will have the chance to practice actions of loving-kindness towards yourself. Make the time today to do something for yourself, to take care of yourself in a loving or nurturing way. Choose something that you don't ordinarily do, but something that could fit into the course of your ordinary day without great effort (for example, going for a massage might be a great gesture of self-care, but would likely require more time and planning). Some examples of self-nurture might include: taking a bubble bath while listening to relaxing music, curling up in front of a fire with a good book, eating dinner by candlelight, buying flowers for yourself, going for a short walk, or making yourself your favorite tea and giving yourself time to enjoy it while you sit in the sunshine.

As you engage in this activity, notice what positive emotions emerge. Take time to savor the experience, be present, and engage as many of your senses as possible.

Make note on your worksheet what you notice about this experience.

> *Example:* Monique typically found herself coming home after work and eating quickly while she watched TV or sat at her computer. She decided that for this exercise, she would stop and buy flowers for herself, something that she loved having in her home, but never thought to do for herself. She put on some favorite music and created an enjoyable dining experience with the flowers and her good china. She took the time to eat slowly and mindfully, while enjoying the taste of her food, the aroma and sight of the flowers, and the sounds of the music. These small gestures elevated her ordinary experience and made her feel that she was worth the extra time and effort. She realized this was how she would treat a good friend, but it never occurred to her to treat herself with this care and attention.

 **EXERCISE SEVEN**

Putting It All Together

Set aside approximately 10 minutes to do this visualization exercise, preferably in the morning if you are able. You can follow along with the guided meditation, or do this on your own following the script below.

Begin by getting into a comfortable position and bring your awareness to your breathing; allow your body to relax and feel supported by the surface that you are sitting upon. Take a few moments to follow your breath as it comes in and as it goes out, finding your natural, comfortable rhythm.

When you are ready, call to mind something or someone for whom you are grateful in your life. This could be a person that you care about, a pet, your health, the fact that you have a house to live in or a job to support you, or anything else in your life that helps you experience a feeling of gratitude. Take some time to let yourself experience the positive effects of gratitude in your body. Notice any ways that your body may shift, relax, feel energized, light, or experience any positive sensations inside.

Now, begin to imagine going through your day, from morning till night, taking this positive feeling with you into your day. As you go through your morning, notice any opportunities you have for bringing this positivity into your actions. How might you speak to yourself or someone else in a loving, caring, kind or attentive way? What small gestures might you do that would be a way of showing kindness, compassion or caring to yourself or someone else?

Notice the times in your day when you tend to get pulled into negativity—whether irritability, anger, frustration, stress or something else. Imagine yourself doing something to generate a more positive emotion. See the numerous choice points throughout your day when this is possible. As you imagine yourself engaging in small actions that bring about positive emotions, allow yourself to fully experience that positivity in your body, and feel its momentum building in you. You may think back to what is most important to you in the ways we explored in Week Two, and notice how small gestures and actions throughout your day help guide you toward being the person you most want to be, and honoring what is most important to you.

Imagine taking a few minutes for yourself during the day to replenish yourself—whether by doing something you love, being in nature, or simply being with yourself for a few minutes in a mindful and caring way. Notice the effect of your actions and your positivity on others around you, and imagine how "contagious" this might be. Allow yourself to experience any positive emotions generated in your body by this exercise, and see if you can be mindful and present with them.

When you are ready, bring your attention back into the room. As you go through your day today, notice how close or far off your day is from what you envisioned.

Record your observations from this exercise on your worksheet.

WRITING ACTIVITY
TIPPING THE SCALE GAME

This week's activity involves a "tipping the scale" game in which for every experience of negativity that arises during the day, your challenge is to create three positive experiences.

One critical piece of the exercise is that the positive experiences must be genuine and authentically felt. Your job is to go through your day, noticing the first signs of negativity arising. Be aware that it is normal for difficult emotions to arise during the day, and it is important for us to honor those feelings, as we discussed in Week Five. However, the point of this activity is to recognize that we can be active participants in creating positive experiences throughout our day, and tipping the scales so that negativity does not take over. So for each negative emotion you experience, try to create three genuine positive experiences for yourself. A few suggestions for doing this include: writing down three things for which you are grateful; stopping and taking a few deep breaths and feeling the calmness that generates; genuinely smiling at someone, or reaching out to them in a kind way; putting your hands on your heart and sending yourself compassion.

At the end of the day, notice what your negative to positive ratio is, and make note of your mood and overall experience of the day.

Example: Janet struggled with mild depression and noticed through previous exercises how easy it was for her thinking to spiral in irrational and unhelpful ways. She was becoming better at catching this and using tools to challenge her irrational thoughts or let her thoughts pass without taking such a strong hold on her. Still, doing this exercise made her aware of her tendency to get pulled into negativity during her day in automatic ways. She found that she had to work to create more positivity in a conscious way, similar to learning and practicing a new skill. Below is an excerpt from her worksheet:

Yelled at my daughter for being slow in the morning, which turned into a minor fight. Afterwards I:

(1) apologized to her for yelling and took some responsibility myself for not leaving myself enough time to get ready;

(2) stopped and put my hands on my heart and sent myself some forgiveness for not being a perfect mother, and also took a moment to appreciate that I was able to apologize and make things right;

(3) took an extra 5 minutes walking from my car into work, breathing in the fresh air and feeling the sun against my skin, allowing myself to "reset" and feel more calm.

Later in the day, I started "beating myself up" for making a mistake on a document at work. Afterwards I:

(1) stopped and made a list of all the things that I do well at work, and took a moment to appreciate this rather than overlook it;

(2) asked a coworker to join me for lunch, rather than isolating myself as I might have otherwise done;

(3) reached out and called my mother-in-law to see how she was feeling, which I know meant a lot to her. Stepping outside of myself and doing something thoughtful for someone else helped me to feel more open and loving, and put my other stressors in perspective.

WEEKLY REFLECTION

♦ I am learning that I have the power and choice to help bring about my own happiness. I understand that this is a skill that can be cultivated and practiced.

♦ Through my daily actions, I can help myself experience positive emotions.

♦ Increasingly, I am noticing small things that I can do each day to take care of others around me, and myself, with compassion and kindness. As I do that, I feel more joy in my life.

♦ As I make space to do what I love and to be more present in my life, I am finding that I have more positive energy. This energy fuels me towards more positivity, and it spreads to others to enrich their lives as well.

SUMMARY OF KEY POINTS

• Happiness is not something that happens to us, but something that we can create each day through our actions. Happiness is much less dictated by our circumstances than it is by the daily behaviors within our control.

• Positive emotions can be cultivated through engaging in a variety of intentional actions including such things as expressing gratitude, practicing acts of kindness, doing activities that we are passionate about, savoring positive experiences, and taking care of ourselves.

• Increasing our positivity can have a beneficial effect not only on how we feel emotionally, but also on our health, our relationships, our ability to see things from a broader perspective, the inner resources that we have to draw on, our creativity, and our success in life.

• Positive emotions carry with them a momentum that can help create an upward spiral in our lives. People who experience three or more positive experiences for roughly every negative experience tend to flourish and thrive and live highly satisfying lives.

Week 6, Exercise 1
BEING IN NATURE

Write down any observations from this exercise. What physical sensations and emotions were you aware of during this experience?

Week 6, Exercise 2

DOING WHAT YOU LOVE AND BEING IN FLOW

Write down any observations from this exercise. What physical sensations and emotions were you aware of experiencing while doing this activity?

Week 6, Exercise 3

GRATITUDE THROUGH ACTION

How did you express gratitude?

How did you feel after doing this?

Other observations:

Week 6, Exercise 4

COMPASSION THROUGH ACTIONS

What action did you take?

What emotions did you experience while doing this, and afterwards?

Other observations:

Week 6, Exercise 5
GENERATING POSITIVE EMOTIONS THROUGH SMALL, RANDOM DISPLAYS OF KINDNESS

List any small, random displays of kindness:

How did it make you feel doing these things?

Week 6, Exercise 6
LOVING-KINDNESS TOWARD ONESELF

What did you do for yourself?

What positive emotions did you experience?

Write down any other observations:

©2017 Beth Kurland, Ph.D.

Week 6, Exercise 7
🔊⟩⟩ PUTTING IT ALL TOGETHER

Part One: Observations from this meditation:

Part Two: How close or far off is your day from what you envisioned?

Week 6, Writing Activity **TIPPING THE SCALE GAME**	
Negative Experience:	**Positive Experience:**
	Positive Experience:
	Positive Experience:
Negative Experience:	**Positive Experience:**
	Positive Experience:
	Positive Experience:
Negative Experience:	**Positive Experience:**
	Positive Experience:
	Positive Experience:
Negative to Positive Ratio:	
Mood and observations from the day:	

©2017 Beth Kurland, Ph.D.

WEEK SEVEN

CULTIVATING POSITIVE EMOTIONS (PART 2)

It's All in Your Head

"With my high stress job at first I was resistant to finding a few minutes in my day to try something new. However, once my doctor told me I had to do something about my high blood pressure, I listened. Setting aside a few minutes in my day has given me a taste of having moments of greater calmness, empathy, and positivity. I have noticed feeling more efficient and effective at work." —HABBAB

As you may have experienced in WEEK SIX, joy, happiness, and positivity are not necessarily products of our circumstances but can be cultivated through the behaviors in which we choose to engage. In this week's chapter you will learn how a positive mindset and your own imagination can also help generate positive emotions.

GOALS AND INTENTIONS FOR THIS WEEK

This week, you will have the opportunity to practice generating positive emotions by using your imagination and thoughts to call up positive experiences. By practicing small shifts in the way you look at things and setting aside a small amount of time to make contact with positive emotions, such as calmness, serenity, and satisfaction, you will experience again how your well-being rests within your own hands.

Why Is This Important?

Positive emotions don't just *feel* good in our bodies; they actually change our physiology in very important, health promoting ways (Rankin, 2014; Childre & Martin, 1999; Childre & Rozman, 2005). Most importantly, research in recent years has shown that we don't have to wait for "good" things to happen to us in order to feel these positive emotions; instead, we can call up positive emotions at will in our minds in order to experience them in our bodies.

I would like to share an example of how this works by discussing the research of the HeartMath® Institute, which has studied the effect of something called "heart rate variability" on health and well-being. As the researchers from HeartMath® describe (Childre & Martin,1999; Childre & Rozman, 2005), our hearts do not beat in a steady, regular rhythm like a metronome (as once believed), but instead change beats moment to moment in an irregular way, due to the influence of the two branches of our autonomic nervous system: the sympathetic nervous system, which accelerates the heart rate (and is responsible for the fight-or-flight response under high stress); and the parasympathetic nervous system, which slows the heart rate (and plays a critical role in turning on what Herbert Benson coined the "relaxation response" (Benson & Klipper, 2000). We need both these branches to survive and function, and the way they work in tandem determines our heart rate variability.

When we experience emotional stress (such as frustration, anger, or anxiety) the sympathetic and parasympathetic branches of the autonomic nervous system are out of sync with one another. When plotted on a graph, this lack of synchrony looks like uneven, jagged lines. HeartMath® researchers compare this discordance to having the right foot on the accelerator of a car and the left foot on the brake, creating a jerky, inefficient ride that puts a lot of wear and tear on the car. On the other hand, when we experience positive emotions, such as appreciation, joy, and love, the two branches of the autonomic nervous system work together in harmony, creating a highly ordered, smooth and harmonious wave-like pattern when graphed. The term used in HeartMath® to describe this physiological shift is "psychophysiological coherence." It turns out that we can create this psychophysiological coherence in our bodies through simple exercises, such as focusing on our breathing, thinking about something we appreciate in our lives, or by calling up happy memories of positive emotions. Our ability to create this coherence in our bodies has far reaching implications. It can lead to greater emotional stability and a sense of well-being; increased mental clarity and improved cognitive functioning; improvements in immune functioning; reduction in anxiety, depression, anger, fatigue, stress and burnout; increases in caring, contentment, gratitude, and peacefulness; and a reduction in numerous health risk factors (HeartMath® Institute).

Cultivating Positive Emotional Experiences

Neuropsychologist Rick Hanson shares groundbreaking work from neuroscientific research in his many books, including *Buddha's Brain* (2009), *Just One Thing* (2011), and *Hardwiring Happiness* (2013) that shows how we can activate different brain states, such as calm, joy, inner peace, compassion, gratitude, and safety, through simple practices in our minds—by in essence recalling positive emotions from past experiences, focusing on them through our imagination, and allowing these positive feeling states to "sink in." Dr. Hanson illuminates how even brief moments of experiencing positive feeling states, repeated over time, change our brain and neural circuitry in positive and profound ways. Dr. Hanson points out that focusing on the good and creating positive experiences is especially important because of the negativity bias of our brains and the tendency of the mind to gravitate toward focusing on unpleasant experiences.

Cultivating positive experiences through simple mental exercises is an important and helpful way to counteract the negativity bias and help make positive emotional experiences a more permanent resource that we can draw on throughout our day (Hanson, 2009; Hanson, 2011; Hanson, 2013). In addition, fostering positive emotions has many benefits for overall wellness: a stronger cardiovascular system that responds better to stress; a stronger immune system; increase in feelings of connectedness and a lower disease risk.

Even at the cellular level, it is thought that positive emotions can prompt cell growth, whereas negative emotions can prompt cell decay (Fredrickson, 2009).

Cultivating a Positive Mindset

Another important way to produce positive emotions is by cultivating a positive mindset. As we have seen, the way we interpret situations and where we choose to focus our attention plays a large role in determining the emotions that we experience. We could be at an amusement park or walking through the woods while thinking about how angry we are with someone who took our parking spot; or we could be at a funeral and feel love and gratitude for the person who died because we are focusing on how they enriched our life. Where we choose to focus our attention matters. In addition, the story that we tell ourselves about a situation and the beliefs that we have about it, can generate negative emotions or positive ones. For example, if the person at the checkout counter snaps at you and you believe it is because he/she has it out for everyone or holds some grudge against you personally, you would likely feel angry. On the other hand, if you believe that something distressing occurred in that person's life that is making them stressed at this moment (e.g., someone they cared about recently died; they are caring for a sick child; their husband just lost his job), you would likely feel neutral, or even compassionate and empathic.

The good news is that even if we do not naturally tend to look at things in a positive way, this is a skill that can be learned, as Martin Seligman, the father of Positive Psychology and major contributor to the field, points out in his book *Learned Optimism* (2006). With practice, we can learn to think differently and change our beliefs and interpretations about situations, and in doing so, we can experience greater positive emotions.

In the following exercises, you will have the opportunity to practice cultivating positive emotions by changing how you look at situations, and by calling up positive emotions using your imagination and memory of past positive experiences. In doing so, you will take one more step towards rewiring your brain for greater wellness and health. Rick Hanson's work on neuroplasticity and "wiring in the good" is a thread throughout these exercises. Several of the exercises were inspired by the year-long course he taught in which I had the privilege of participating (Hanson, 2014).

The first two exercises, and the sixth exercise, are inspired by Dr. Robert Brooks, who was my mentor during my internship training at McLean Hospital in Belmont,

Massachusetts. Dr. Brooks is a psychologist and internationally renowned teacher and author on the subject of resilience. He is a leading expert on helping parents and teachers cultivate resilience in children, and he has written numerous books on the subject. Among the many subjects he studies are the concepts of developing empathy by walking in someone else's shoes, and nurturing "islands of competence" by noticing, developing, accepting, and celebrating children's accomplishments and successes (Brooks & Goldstein, 2002). In addition, he and Dr. Goldstein, in their book, *Raising Resilient Children* (2002) write that one of the important qualities of a resilient mindset is the ability to face hardships and obstacles by viewing them as challenges to overcome rather than stressors to avoid. We will use these ideas to help us cultivate positive emotional experiences.

EXERCISE ONE

Developing Empathy - Walking in Someone Else's Shoes

This exercise is designed to generate positive emotions (specifically empathy) in a situation in which you might not otherwise experience it, by learning to look differently at someone else by imagining that you are standing in their shoes. I first learned this exercise from Dr. Brooks during my internship years, when I worked with parents and helped them learn to react with more empathy toward their children.

To begin, take a moment to call to mind someone toward whom you now feel, or recently felt angry or irritated. Ideally, pick a neutral person, or someone that you care about. For example, it could be a partner, spouse, child, parent or friend whom you were upset with, or perhaps a stranger, such as a person who cut ahead of you in line at the store, or the cashier who spoke to you in a rude tone. For the purpose of this exercise, try to avoid choosing someone who has deeply hurt or harmed you in a significant way.

Once you have a person and a situation in mind, take a moment to remember how you felt when the event occurred. Now begin to put yourself in that person's shoes for a moment. Truly imagine what it might be like to be in their body, in their mind, and in their life—in essence, what it would be like to be them. If it is a stranger you are thinking of, let yourself imagine different possibilities for what their life might be like. See if from this perspective, you can understand perhaps better than before why they acted the way they did. It is not important that you agree or disagree with their words or actions, or whether they were "right or wrong"; what matters is that you get some sense of where they were coming from and how it felt to be them in that moment.

Experiencing empathy does not mean you have to agree with the other person's behavior; however, see if you can imagine the situation from their perspective. In doing so, see if you might be able to experience some compassion and some empathy toward them. Notice how your body reacts as you call up these feelings. What shifts or changes in you when you are able to feel empathic? How might this inform future interactions?

As you go through your day today, try to step into other people's shoes and imagine what it feels like to be them. Notice how this affects your feelings and your behavior throughout the day. Record your observations in your workbook.

Example: Frank (introduced in Week One), saw this as an opportunity to practice empathy toward his teenage son. He thought about a conflict they had the previous night, in which Frank was upset because his son hadn't completed a chore he had asked him to complete earlier in the day. When he put himself in his son's shoes he imagined what it was like getting up early and sitting through six hours of classes, which for the most part were not very exciting. Then he imagined going to sports practice, and coming home to three hours of homework, including studying for two tests the following day. He imagined feeling anxious and stressed, as he knew his son often felt. Then he imagined an adult yelling at him, making demands, and telling him there was more he needed to do, right NOW. He could understand, from this perspective, that this might not feel very good. His own frustration shifted as he engaged in this exercise, and he noticed that it was replaced by a feeling of empathy and understanding. This didn't mean that his son was going to be able to skip his chores, but Frank could envision approaching his son in a different way, perhaps by sitting down with him and seeing if they could agree on a time by which his son could complete the chore before the night was through.

Example: Marilyn was driving home from work, seemingly minding her own business, when a car on the other side of the road started to honk loudly. She looked over instinctively, and realized that the driver was not beeping at her, but at someone else. However, as she looked over, the driver of the other vehicle held up her middle finger at her and gave her a nasty look. Normally, something like this would evoke rage and distress for Marilyn and would set off a stress response that could last for a very long time. However, she saw this as an opportunity to practice empathy. She took some slow, deep breaths and began to imagine what this person's life might be like to resort to such behavior. She wondered what conditions this person grew up in, and imagined that perhaps she didn't have nurturing, supportive parents to help her feel secure as a child. Or perhaps she was bullied as a teenager and experienced the world as an unsafe and threatening place. She envisioned that this person must have had some very painful experiences in her life to behave in such a way to an innocent stranger.

As she thought these things, her own anger began to soften and dissipate, and she noticed feeling some compassion for this person who may have lived through difficult circumstances. While that clearly did not excuse the driver's behavior in any way, Marilyn was able to experience some empathy which enabled her to let the experience go, creating a greater feeling of well-being and ease in her own body.

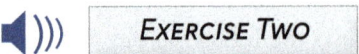

EXERCISE TWO

Finding "Islands of Competence" in Ourselves and Others

It is easy to see faults in ourselves and others, and often much harder to find and focus on what is good and well and right. Today we will focus on recognizing strengths and areas of competency in ourselves and those around us. Dr. Brooks was instrumental in teaching this concept to me, and it is a cornerstone of his work on resiliency. You can do this exercise as a mind-body experience, or if you prefer, as a writing exercise.

Begin by thinking about someone you know well, perhaps someone who does not always see their own strengths. Take some time to identify their "islands of competence."

- What do they do well?
- What gifts do they bring to others just by being themselves?

– In what ways have they contributed and do they now contribute to those around them?

– Are there specific achievements or accomplishments that they have made?

– What natural talents and abilities do they have? What personal qualities do they have that you appreciate (e.g., are they funny, intelligent, caring, friendly, trustworthy, etc.?).

As you take the time to identify their "islands of competence," allow yourself to pause and feel a sense of appreciation growing inside yourself for these qualities that they have. Notice how that feels in your own body as you take the time to notice and appreciate these qualities; you might even imagine sending this feeling of appreciation to them, and letting them know you value these qualities in them.

When you are ready, imagine someone, or more than one person, thinking of you and seeing your "islands of competence."

– What would they say, notice, and appreciate about you?

– What would others say that you do well, and/or what qualities would others see in you that they might admire?

Sometimes it is easier to see our own "islands of competence" through other people's eyes.

Now see if you can look at yourself through your own eyes and embrace and appreciate all of the wonderful qualities about yourself, all of the things that you do well, all of the ways that you are unique and special, or ways that you contribute to those around you. Some people may have a more difficult time with this, and if so, that is OK. Still, see if you can find at least one genuine quality about yourself that you can truly appreciate.

Pause and allow yourself to feel a growing sense of appreciation or gratitude towards yourself. Imagine nurturing this in yourself, seeing your own strengths grow, along with your sense of appreciation. Send yourself compassion, caring, and gratitude as you allow yourself to focus on your strengths.

As you go through your day today, write down everything you notice about other "people's islands of competence," (try to see the good in them) as well as your own. See if you can recognize and appreciate the things that you do well today, small or large, and acknowledge yourself for this. Be sure to write down what you observe on your worksheet.

Example: Channah, introduced in Week Six, found that this exercise was another small step towards her creation of some "positive momentum" in her week. She had no problem identifying "islands of competence" in another person (she chose her sister for the purpose of this exercise). She had a close relationship with her sister, and felt a deep appreciation for her sister's warmth and caring, and her ability to juggle a career and be a loving mother. Calling up feelings of appreciation for her sister made her feel a little "lighter" inside. When Channah imagined what her sister might say about her "islands of competence," she knew her sister would probably say she was creative, artistic, and had a real knack for figuring out how things worked, for fixing things, and for making things. She knew that her sister appreciated her sense of humor and the way that she had a "listening ear" when her sister was upset. She imagined hearing her sister saying these things to her, which allowed her to acknowledge some of these qualities in herself. Channah was aware of how easy it was for her to find fault with herself for every little thing, and how rare it was for her to see the good in herself. Spending a few minutes doing this exercise, as well as recognizing the good in her sister, helped lift her mood. This positive emotional experience gave her energy to bring into other activities in her day.

Wiring-In Serenity

This next exercise will be an opportunity to replenish yourself through a mini vacation using your imagination. Your imagination can be a powerful tool for turning on your relaxation response and creating feelings of peacefulness and well-being. Learning to use it for this purpose can be restorative for your body and mind. Follow along with the audio if you are able, or use the script that follows to guide you.

Allow yourself to get into a comfortable position, either lying down, or sitting up. Begin by taking some slow, deep breaths, following each in breath and out breath, noticing the rise and fall of your belly. Find a comfortable rhythm of breathing, and for a few cycles of breathing, see if you can allow the length of your inhalation and exhalation to be the same (that is, if you breathe in to a count of three, breathe out to a count of three). Continue in this manner for a few minutes.

Now, with each exhalation, give your body permission to let go of any stress and tension it might be holding, by allowing it to ease out with each outbreath. Take some time to scan your body from head to toe, noticing any places that might feel tense or tight, and inviting some breath into those places to create a little bit of space.

When you are ready, call to mind a beautiful, safe, serene place, and begin to see this place in your mind and envision yourself there. It could be a place where you have been before; it could be a place where you would like to go; or it could be an imagined place in your mind. As you see yourself in this serene place, allow yourself to use all of your senses to fully experience being there.

Take a moment to look around and notice the sights, colors, and textures. Listen to the sounds of this place—birds singing, leaves rustling, music playing, the sound of stillness, or something else. Smell any aromas in this special place—perhaps flowers or fresh cut grass. Notice any sensations against your skin—perhaps the feeling of sunshine caressing you, or a gentle breeze blowing, or sand under your feet. Notice what it feels like to be in this safe, serene, beautiful place. Imagine what you might be doing there—perhaps sitting in a chair, lying down, walking, exploring. The more real you can make this place in your mind, the more your body will be able to experience it as if you were there.

As you take in this experience, feel a sense of peace and relaxation spreading throughout your whole body. Be with this feeling, or whatever feeling is present for you, as long as you like, and when you are ready, bring your awareness back into the room.

Example: Habbab decided to try this exercise during his lunch break. He had a high stress job as the manager of a large corporation, and worked long hours. His doctor had expressed concern at his last visit about rising blood pressure, and Habbab was open to trying different ways to help his body relax and de-stress. He liked the idea of having a "mini vacation" to help him reset in the middle of the day, and found this exercise very enjoyable. He was able to get into a relaxed state fairly quickly by imagining himself at the ocean, where he used to go every summer as a child. He found that when he returned to work after doing this exercise, he was more energized, focused, and efficient, so taking 5–10 minutes out of his day was well worth it.

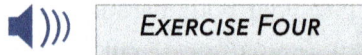

EXERCISE FOUR

Wiring-In Calmness

Being able to summon positive emotions is an important tool for countering the stress response. While there are many benefits to being able to experience positive emotions when we are not under stress, it is also beneficial to be able to access certain emotions, such as feeling calm during stressful times, to increase our resiliency and coping. For the purpose of this exercise, we will practice calling forth feelings of calmness in the context of stressful or challenging situations. It may be helpful to follow along with the audio for this exercise.

To begin, call to mind a time in your life when you felt calm amidst a stressful situation. If you cannot think of such a time, see if you can recall a time when someone you know was able to remain calm during a stressful situation, and imagine what that felt like for them. You could also call to mind a fictional character, if that is easier. The important aspect of this exercise is to have the opportunity to imagine and experience the calmness now in your own body, even as you imagine the stress of a situation around and outside of you. You might think about a time when you remained calm during an argument, or were calm when a child was upset, anxious or angry. You might think about a time when you were calm during a test, during a stressful day at work, or when you were trying to solve a challenging problem.

As you think about that situation, bring your awareness into your body and notice where you feel the calmness in your body, and specifically what sensations you feel in your body. Allow that feeling of calmness to become familiar to you, and stay with it for several minutes. If it helps, you might think about the image from Week Five of the strong tree with long roots that anchor it deeply into the earth. Picture those roots holding the tree stable and secure in the ground, even as storms howl above. Another image that might be helpful is imagining yourself in the eye of a hurricane, that calm center of the storm. Find that place of calmness within yourself, and be present to it. Know that you can call up this feeling when you need it because it is already within you.

To assist you in doing this, see if you can think of an image, word, symbol, sensation or something else that comes to mind that can act as a cue to remind you of this calm feeling as you are going through your day. For example, you might feel the sensation of your feet planted firmly on the ground and imagine those strong stable roots beneath you as a way to call up a feeling of calmness amidst a storm. Come up with your own cue that is meaningful to you and know that you can use this to help bring you back to this place of calm.

As you go through your day today, see if you can practice using the cue that you selected, to help you summon the calm feeling and anchor it within you. Try to do this several times during the day. Don't worry about waiting until you are feeling stressed to practice this; sometimes it is easier at first to practice when you are not feeling a high level of stress so that it becomes familiar and easier to apply during times of stress.

Example: Melonie thought about her ability to remain calm and centered when her son, who had an intense temperament, was having a meltdown. During those times, Melonie was able to maintain a healthy perspective and recognize that "this too shall pass" and that her son was OK and would learn to regulate his own emotions if she could remain a calm, loving presence, go about her business, and not give the meltdown undue attention.

Melonie found it interesting to note that she had much more difficulty remaining calm when little things in her own life didn't go as expected. As she focused on reexperiencing (through memory) these moments of calm with her son, she had a clear sense in her own body of how that calmness felt. The image that came to her mind was of herself in the center of a clear, glass pyramid, that protected her from the storms around her. It was safe inside the pyramid, and she was able to experience that feeling of safety inside her body. She decided that she would use the image of a pyramid to help her anchor the feeling of calmness in her body. Throughout the day, she visualized the image of the pyramid, and when she did so, she was able to experience that calm and safety within her body.

EXERCISE FIVE

Wiring-In Satisfaction

In the previous week's chapter we practiced experiencing gratitude through our actions. The feeling of satisfaction is a kind of variation on gratitude; it is that feeling of non-striving, of acceptance of things as they are in this moment, of not needing things to be different in order to feel OK, of being content with ourselves and what we have right now. Our culture gives us such strong messages in the media and elsewhere that if we only acquire this one additional item (a new car, a new hair product, an item of clothing) and change something about ourselves (lose weight, dress differently, have less wrinkles) we will be happy. Satisfaction runs counter to this and is all about embracing a sense of "OK-ness" and inner peace just as things are. That doesn't mean that we shouldn't have goals and aspirations, but that we can appreciate this moment without needing to have reached those additional goals.

Set aside approximately 10 minutes for this exercise when you won't be interrupted. You can choose to follow the guided audio meditation, or use the script below to go at your own pace.

Begin by finding a comfortable seated position, feeling your back straight (if you are able to do this seated) and your feet planted firmly on the ground. Take some slow, deliberate breaths in and out through your nose.

See if you can recall a time in your life when you felt perfectly content in the moment, when you weren't trying to achieve anything, when you felt very present, when you didn't have a feeling of needing to "do" anything, but could just be as you are. Perhaps this was a time when you were on vacation, or out in nature, sitting on your porch on a sunny day, or perhaps a time when you were a child playing outdoors or running in the sand. If nothing comes to mind, see if you can take yourself to such a time now and feel that in this moment everything is OK. Give yourself permission to let go of your "to do" list for a few minutes, to let go of needing to be or look or act a certain way, to let go of needing to do anything for anyone else. Even though you may acknowledge that there are real challenges in your life or problems to solve, see if you can call up a feeling of "OK-ness" in **this** moment. If you are recalling a memory of feeling that way, put yourself back there now. Take some time to experience in your body what this feeling of satisfaction is like. You may choose to combine this with a feeling of gratitude for whatever blessings and goodness you have in your life now.

Now, when you are ready, take a moment to imagine yourself as a newborn who just came into the world. How might you view this newborn; how might you hold this newborn; how might you feel towards this newborn? See if you can experience a sense of this newborn as perfect just as they are. If this is difficult for you to imagine about yourself, see if you can imagine someone you care about as a newborn coming into the world. Can you experience a sense of that baby as perfect just as he or she is? Can you sense a feeling of unconditional love and acceptance toward that baby?

Holding onto that feeling, see if you can bring that feeling to yourself now. Can you experience—even some small part of yourself—that despite your imperfections you are OK just the way you are. If you are able to experience this, notice how it feels in your body, this sense of "I am OK just as I am." If you are having difficulty experiencing this, see if you can go experience this for someone you care about, and allow this feeling to become familiar within you.

When you are ready, bring your awareness back into the room.

Example: Janet, from Week Six, found the first part of this exercise easier than the second part. She recalled the times when she was younger and would go hiking with the dog in the woods near her house. She remembered feeling completely at peace when she was hiking, no matter what might have been bothering her before the walk. When she was in the woods, she was somehow able to be fully present to what was in front of her without feeling the need to accomplish anything or to change anything. She was able to call up this feeling easily, and enjoyed how that sense of satisfaction felt in her body. She noticed her muscles relaxing and unwinding. Janet was able to experience a sense of being enough just the way she was as a newborn, but had a harder time extending these feelings to her adult self. When she tried to do this, she was aware of thoughts arising such as "yes but you really need to quit smoking and lose weight—you know that isn't good for you, and you've got to stop making so many careless mistakes at work—your boss isn't going to be happy with you." When these thoughts arose, she tried to let them pass by, without getting pulled into them. She went back to focusing on that feeling of unconditional acceptance of herself as an infant. She then found it helpful to say to herself "of course I have imperfections and things I want to work on now in my life, but I'm OK anyway. I have enough. I am enough." She found that she could embrace these words, even on some small level for a few seconds at a time, and saying this to herself helped her to relax inside.

EXERCISE SIX

Wiring-In Resilience Through a Positive Mindset

In their book, *Raising Resilient Children* (2002), Dr. Brooks and Dr. Goldstein wrote that one of the characteristics of a resilient mindset is to recognize mistakes and setbacks as experiences from which to learn and grow.

For today's exercise, see if you can call to mind a difficult situation that occurred in your life in which you were able to step back and find some good in it, or create some meaning from it, or turn it into a learning experience in some helpful way. Perhaps it was a time when you experienced a rejection, didn't get a job you wanted, had an injury or sickness, had an unexpected disappointment, or made a mistake in some way. If you can't think of anything, you can think of someone else you know who handled a challenging experience in a positive way, and imagine what that person felt like. Alternatively, perhaps you can imagine how you might handle a past challenging situation *now* in such a way that you could find a "silver lining" in your experience. Some examples include: a star, teenage athlete who was injured and could not play his sport but decided to help coach his team; a father who was laid off and appreciated the opportunity to spend more time with his children; a woman who was fired from her job and saw it as a chance to re-evaluate her work environment and choose a less pressured work setting; a person who received a speeding ticket and chose to see it as a "wake up call" to slow down in her life.

Once you have a suitable situation in mind, allow yourself to focus on how you rose above this experience to find something positive in it, or learned from it in some way, that allowed you to move past it. Notice how you looked at the situation in a way that was helpful. Focus on this feeling of resilience inside of you, the inner strength that allowed you to face a hard situation and get through it. Let yourself feel empowered, knowing that you not only got through a difficult situation, but also were able to have a positive mindset to help guide you.

As you feel that inner strength and resiliency within you, imagine being able to draw on this again in other challenges that may come your way. Recognize that you have a powerful tool—your mind—to help you see the value, meaning, and knowledge gained by overcoming challenges in your life.

> *Example:* Miriam, a high school student, immediately thought of a recent challenging situation that she had experienced. She had been involved in theater and acting classes for several years, which she very much enjoyed, and she had tried out for the school play, in which she believed she would earn a role. To her dismay, she was not offered a part, while many of her friends (some with less experience) were offered roles. This was extremely upsetting and disappointing to her. When she reflected back on this experience, she realized that despite her disappointment, she had made the decision shortly after this to try out for the debate team instead. She had told herself at the time that just because she didn't get into the play, this shouldn't stop her from trying to pursue other things. Going through this exercise, Miriam experienced a sense of inner strength and resilience that she hadn't realized was there. Thinking about the experience now, she felt empowered and proud that she hadn't let one disappointment get in the way of going after other things she wanted. She realized that this feeling of inner resilience from this experience could be helpful to call up in the future when she might experience disappointment.

Putting It All Together

In this mind-body exercise you will have the chance to put together everything you have learned this week and imagine applying it in your life. It might be best to follow along with the audio if possible.

To begin, imagine that you are able to watch scenes from your week played on a TV screen in front of you. At first, allow yourself to see the week unfold before you by watching old "reruns"—that is, by seeing how you have behaved in the past. Notice, in particular, old, automatic patterns of behavior and tendencies to get pulled into negativity that may not serve you well.

Once you have a sense of what has not worked so well, pause for a moment and set an intention for yourself that going forward you are committed to building opportunities to cultivate positive emotional experiences through your thoughts and the use of your imagination. See yourself going through each day and practicing asking yourself what another person may be feeling, before you react in a situation. See yourself pausing and experiencing a feeling of empathy, and notice how it feels in your body to experience this emotion.

When you have a problem or challenge that arises during the week (and you can take a moment to imagine what a typical one might be), imagine that you have a special telescope that you can look through that allows you to look at the situation from a broader perspective, and allows you to see some meaning, or lesson, or some way of viewing this not as on obstacle but as a challenge that you can handle.

Notice how your week feels when you focus your attention on your strengths and the things that you do well, and the strengths of others, rather than focusing on shortcomings. Take some time to picture how your week looks and feels when you see the good in yourself and others. Imagine taking some time during your week to include some "mini-vacations." Notice the effect that visualizing yourself in a special, safe, and peaceful place has on your mood, energy, and behavior during your day. Imagine having moments during your day when you can feel a sense of satisfaction and "enough-ness" just where you are, without needing to change anything about yourself or your life.

This altered perspective might only last a few seconds or minutes but simply notice how you might help to create those moments of satisfaction, and how it feels in your body to do so. Picture yourself practicing your cue to call up a feeling of calmness in your body throughout the week. Imagine a time during your week when a typical stressor occurs, and see yourself using your cue to remain calm. Allow yourself to feel this calmness in your body now.

As an important part of this exercise, take some time to write on your worksheet how you might incorporate each of these skills into your week. Be as specific as possible.

Example: Janet came up with the following ideas after this exercise:

- At the first signs of getting upset with my daughter or husband, take a moment to stop and imagine walking in their shoes, seeing the world through their eyes, before I react.

- Start my day by acknowledging and appreciating at least one positive thing about myself, whether it be something I'm good at, or a quality others appreciate in me.

- In the waiting room on Wednesday morning before my medical procedure, take at least 5 minutes to go to a peaceful place in my mind, to help me relax.

- Right before my work presentation Friday morning, take a moment to visualize my tree with roots, calling up a calm and centered feeling in my body.

WRITING ACTIVITY

POSITIVITY BOX

For this week's activity, you will make a special box that you can fill with things that evoke positive emotions. The box can be whatever size you choose as long as it can hold either the things themselves, or a representation of the things, which allow you to call up positive emotions. Some examples include the following: favorite inspirational songs put together on a CD from your playlist, a poem that inspires you, words or quotes written on index cards, a seashell from the ocean, your favorite scented candle, a list of things you are grateful for, a special card you received from someone, a picture of a beautiful, peaceful place that you would love to visit, a certificate you earned that you are proud of, or photographs. The idea is to put together a collection of items that can be pulled from your box, whenever you choose, to help you call forth positive emotions.

As a variation of this, a friend of mine started what she calls a "smile file" on her computer. Every time something positive happens or someone says something nice or meaningful to her, she writes it down in a file on her computer. Then when she is feeling down or feels like she is being pulled into negativity, she opens the file and reads what she has written to help lift her mood.

> *Example*: Channah decided to fill her box with positive things about herself written on decorative note cards—including accomplishments, qualities that she likes about herself, and things that other people appreciate in her. At the suggestion of her therapist, she asked close friends and family members to each write a card for her box with something they love, appreciate or admire about her. Having these cards to look at during the day helped her feel uplifted when she realized she was getting pulled into negativity.

WEEKLY REFLECTION

- I choose to seek out and create positive emotions for myself to experience today. As I do this, I realize that I am taking care of my body and myself in a profound way, as well as caring for the people around me.

- I am looking for the good in myself and others today. I know it is easy to see the negatives, but I choose to see what is good in myself and others, and to appreciate this.

- Even though I am not perfect by any means and may work on ways to improve myself, I choose to accept myself in this moment just as I am.

- Although I have goals and desires and things I might want to have, or things I might want to change, I accept that in this moment I have enough, and I allow myself to acknowledge the blessings in my life and the feeling of satisfaction that comes with that.

- I choose to practice ways to feel calm and relaxed inside of myself. Taking even a few minutes a day to do this can help me to "reset," feel replenished, and be more resilient to stress when it arises.

KEY SUMMARY POINTS

- Just as we can cultivate positive emotions through our actions, we can also cultivate positive emotions through our imagination and our thinking. Calling up positive emotions, even for short periods of time, can have significant and far-reaching health benefits. It changes the physiology within our bodies in health-promoting ways.

- One way of helping ourselves to experience positive emotions is by thinking about images or memories that enable us to recall specific positive feeling in our bodies. We can also focus on things that we appreciate in ourselves and others in order to call up positive emotions. By training our minds to remember and see the good around us, we also allow this experience to be felt in our bodies. When we activate this mind-body connection, we promote health and wellness on a mental, emotional, and physiological level.

- Another way to experience positive emotions is to change the way we think about or interpret situations. For example, when we are able to stand in someone else's shoes and see things from their perspective, or when we are able to find some meaning or lesson or positive challenge in a difficult situation, we cultivate positive emotional experiences that enhance our resiliency and counter negativity.

Week 7, Exercise 1
DEVELOPING EMPATHY—
WALKING IN SOMEONE ELSE'S SHOES

Observations from putting yourself in someone else's shoes:

What might it feel like to be that other person?

How does this perspective shift or change your own feelings and behaviors throughout the day?

Week 7, Exercise 2
FINDING "ISLANDS OF COMPETENCE" IN OURSELVES AND OTHERS

Identify and describe someone else's "islands of competence":

Identify and describe your own "islands of competence":

What did you observe from this exercise?

During the day, write down all of the good that you see in others:

Write down all of the good that you see in yourself:

©2017 Beth Kurland, Ph.D.

Week 7, Exercise 3
WIRING-IN SERENITY

🔊)))

Write down any observations from this meditation:

How might you use this exercise in the future? In what way might it be helpful to you?

Week 7, Exercise 4
WIRING-IN CALMNESS

Write down your observations from this meditation:

What cue did you come up with that you might use to bring back this calm feeling?

Situation	Able to practice cue (yes/no)	Observations

©2017 Beth Kurland, Ph.D.

Week 7, Exercise 5
WIRING-IN SATISFACTION

🔊)))

Write down any observations from this meditation.

How might you use this exercise in the future? In what way might it be helpful to you?

©2017 Beth Kurland, Ph.D.

Week 7, Exercise 6
WIRING-IN RESILIENCE THROUGH A POSITIVE MINDSET

Difficult situation:

How might you look at this situation in a way that helps you feel more resilient? What inner strengths might you draw on?

How might you use this feeling of resilience or empowerment to help you in future situations?

©2017 Beth Kurland, Ph.D.

Week 7, Exercise 7

🔊))) **PUTTING IT ALL TOGETHER**

Observations from this meditation:

Write down how you might incorporate each of these skills into your week? Be as specific as possible.

©2017 Beth Kurland, Ph.D.

Week 7, Writing Activity
POSITIVITY BOX

Take a few minutes to write down how you might use your box to help you during the weeks ahead:

©2017 Beth Kurland, Ph.D.

WEEK EIGHT

PUTTING IT ALL TOGETHER

Creating Your Personal Wellness Action Plan

"I have always tended to buy self-help books and start to read them, but never actually put any of the ideas into action. Having these concrete exercises and some guidance in putting together a long term plan for myself has really motivated me to follow through and take my well-being into my own hands." —BOB

GOALS AND INTENTIONS FOR THIS WEEK

THIS WEEK'S CHAPTER WILL HELP YOU to practice combining the various skills from this book and utilize them in your daily life. You will develop a wellness action plan for how you will continue to practice and utilize the skills learned to bring them into your life.

Why Is This Important?

In order to learn new skills and, in essence, rewire your brain for greater well-being, you need a plan of action that will allow you to integrate everything that you have learned and, most importantly, apply it on a daily basis, so that lasting change can occur. It is helpful to recognize that this action plan can be individualized to fit your needs and your lifestyle, and that what you need for balance and well-being may differ greatly from other people around you.

There are multiple ways to think about putting all of this material together. One way to think of this is to imagine each of the chapters and exercises in this book as steps in a dance. Each step in the dance can stand on its own, but when we learn to put the steps together in new and different ways, we can create a larger, more coherent pattern of movement and behavior that gives us greater choices and flexibility for handling life's challenges. Practicing each of the individual steps is critically important, but eventually we can listen to the music and decide whether there is a foxtrot or waltz or tango or rap playing, and move accordingly by stringing together multiple steps based on what the music is calling for.

Situations often present in complex ways so if we are comfortable with individual skills or "steps," we can combine them to help us most effectively. When feeling stressed for example, one may stop and breathe, recognize irrational thoughts starting to form, choose to focus on more rational or helpful thoughts, and then call up feelings of gratitude in order to shift into a more positive state of well-being.

As a personal example of this, one day during the winter while I was at work, I received a phone call from my husband, who said he was on his way to the hospital emergency room because he had fallen while skiing and seriously injured his leg. He said that because of the injury, he was unable to walk. After I talked to him on the phone, I could feel myself starting to get pulled into a spiral of negativity and panic, but my sister, whom I called for support, wisely reminded me to use the tools that I teach.

I took a few minutes to practice the tree exercise (in Week Five) to ground myself and call up a sense of strength and stability. I then gave myself a few minutes to be present with my feelings and to simply acknowledge them. As I did this, I became aware of my negative thinking, and in particular, the tendency of my mind to run wild into the future with all kinds of imagined fears. This became an opportunity to rein my thinking back into the present moment to remind myself that at this time, I was "fundamentally OK," (a phrase that Rick Hanson uses in his teachings) (Hanson, 2014), and so was my husband, despite his injured leg. I then turned my attention to things I could be grateful for: my husband's head was not injured in the ski accident, this was not life threatening and there are many supportive people in our lives available to help.

Taking the few minutes to do this enabled me to cope with this challenging situation in a much more helpful, and less reactive way. Thankfully, my husband was able to recover fully from his injury, and it was not even as bad as I had originally feared.

Staying Balanced

In addition to considering the exercises and chapters of the book as steps in a dance, another helpful way to think about maintaining our well-being over time is to use an analogy of balancing the chemicals of a swimming pool. In order to maintain the health of a swimming pool, one needs to take water samples on a weekly basis and see whether certain levels of chemicals are too high, too low, or just right. If the alkalinity or PH or chlorine levels are off, you can add what is needed so that the water is balanced. When the water is well balanced, algae and bacteria cannot grow; however, when the water is out of balance these things are much more likely to show up and present problems. So too, when we are feeling balanced, we are less likely to react with a full out stress response to a small trigger; yet when we are depleted or out of balance, even the smallest problem might set us off, making us more susceptible to negativity taking over.

We need to assess and inventory our lives on a daily, weekly, or monthly basis to determine what is out of balance and what we most need in order to come back into balance. For some people, noticing their negative thinking may be where attention is most needed; for other people, learning to create space for sadness or anger may be what is called for; for still others, cultivating positive emotions may be most essential. When we are aware of what within us needs the most attention, we can tailor our action plan to meet those needs.

Developing a Personalized Plan

Some other analogies that might be helpful in thinking about integrating the skills from this book include the idea of developing a business plan, for those who are business minded, or a training plan, for those who resonate with a fitness model. All the tools in the world are of no use if you don't use them. Having a short and long-term plan that takes into account your specific lifestyle and needs is more likely to give you the motivation and structure required to make the new skills a regular part of your life. It may help to start small and pick some goals that you know you can achieve, and then build on these. For some of my patients, who work full time and have young children, setting a mindfulness bell that goes off on their phone every hour is a great way to begin to incorporate mindfulness and greater awareness into their lives and can remind them to focus on what is important. For some business executives with high stress jobs, planning a three minute breathing space several times throughout their day can help to reset their automatic stress patterns. For other people, going on a mindful walk on a daily basis or keeping an emotion diary or gratitude journal may be a great place to start.

While this book offers a myriad of tools and strategies for improving your life, I encourage you to decide on the approach that will best work for you, and develop a plan that involves small, achievable goals (you will have an opportunity to develop this below). You may find it most helpful to go back and focus on one chapter of the book at a time, or you may benefit from trying to integrate multiple skills more quickly.

Move to the rhythm of your own dance. Remember that changing automatic habits and establishing new patterns and pathways in your brain takes continued practice, like learning any new skill. You know best what you need, so listen to your own inner voice in your journey ahead. Below you will find some exercises to guide you.

EXERCISE ONE

Self-Test

Take the following self-test to determine what skills might be most helpful for you to focus on going forward, and as a first step in developing your personalized wellness plan. You may think of this exercise as testing the water quality in your personal swimming pool, to find out what is in balance and what is out of balance.

Rate the following fourteen statements on a scale of 1–7, where 1 reflects statements with which you strongly disagree, and 7 represents statements with which you strongly agree.

You will notice that each pair of questions is similar, but phrased differently. That is intentional, so just answer each question as accurately as possible without worrying about the questions before it. **This questionnaire works best if you answer all of the questions with an *a* first, and then go back and answer all of the questions with a *b*.**

1a. I am very aware of when I begin to experience stress. I can notice the early warning signs of stress in my body, my emotions and my thinking.

1b. Stress often sneaks up on me and takes me over before I even recognize that it is there. I can easily go from zero to 100 when situations trigger me, and I do this fairly automatically, as if on "automatic pilot."

2a. I have a strong sense of what is important to me in my work and personal life and I use these values to help guide me and motivate me toward behaving in ways that help me be my best self.

2b. I don't have a strong sense of what is most important to me at work and in my personal life, and I struggle to find the motivation to change my behavior for the better.

3a. I am able to be present during daily activities and when I am interacting with others. I am focused on what I am doing in the moment and am not often distracted by my own thinking.

3b. I tend to find myself in the past or future more often than the present. My mind wanders off frequently and I might not even realize that I am not paying attention to what is happening in the present moment.

4a. I am very aware of my negative thinking and irrational thoughts when they arise, and I am able to use tools to put things in perspective and not get swept away by these thoughts.

4b. My negative thinking can overtake me easily and before I know it I am caught up in a cascade of negative and irrational thoughts that tend to snowball.

5a. I am able to identify what I am feeling fairly easily and, when faced with difficult emotions, I am able to allow myself to feel them.

5b. I am often unaware of my feelings and when uncomfortable feelings arise they tend to either pull me into an emotional spiral, or I tend to try and push them away.

6a. There are things that I do on a regular basis that help me to experience feelings of joy, gratitude, compassion and loving-kindness.

6b. I believe that happiness is determined mostly by outside circumstances that happen to me, and I don't feel that there is much I can do to feel happier or more joyful.

7a. I am able to call up positive feelings such as calmness, peace, and empathy and tend to have a positive mindset to help me when challenges arise.

7b. I have a hard time experiencing positive emotions and I find myself stuck in negative feeling states.

Scoring: Subtract the score of question 1a from the score of question 1b, keeping in mind that you might get a negative number. (For example, if your score was 3 for question 1a, and 6 for question 1b, you would end up with a –3 for that set of questions. If you scored 6 for question 3a and scored 2 for question 3b you would end up with a 4 for this pair of questions.)

Do this for each of the pairs of questions.

Each numbered question corresponds to a chapter/week in the book. The lower the number, the more it suggests that this might be an area on which to focus, while the higher the combined number, the more this is an area of strength or balance for you.

Look at the range of numbers that you end up with to determine where your high and low numbers fall. (In the example above, a minus 3 corresponding to Week One might be a relatively low number, suggesting that this would be a place where you could benefit from going back to that chapter and working on the skills outlined there. In contrast, the score of 4 in the example above, corresponding to Week Three, would represent an area of relative strength or balance for you that would require less practice.

Exercise Two

Smoke Detectors and Fire Extinguishers

The purpose of this exercise is to identify strategies that you can proactively put in place to help make your life go more smoothly, as well as to recognize "emergency" measures that you can call on when you are caught in a flood of overwhelming feelings or thoughts, to prevent negativity from spiraling. Think of the first set of skills as similar to a smoke detector, which alerts you at the first sign of a fire, gives you peace of mind and helps to create a sense of security and safety. Think of the second set of skills as a fire extinguisher, which can be used to put a fire out once it starts to burn out of control.

Take some time to review the exercises in each chapter of this book. Make a note of those that worked best to help you become aware of, prevent, and manage stress and difficult emotions, notice negative thinking, and cultivate positive emotions. These are your smoke detector strategies. Now, write down those exercises that would work best for you when you are overwhelmed with intense emotions (your fire extinguisher strategies).

Don't be limited by the exercises in this book. Think about the tools you already use to calm yourself and self-regulate when you are very upset, angry, anxious, or stressed. If it helps, take some time to imagine yourself on your best day, and notice what you are doing to help make it a good day. Imagine yourself at your worst, and ask yourself what it is that you most need to do in that moment to help yourself. Taking the time to think about this now, when you are calm, can help you remember to use your tools on a daily basis as well as during times of "crisis."

Example: Bob decided that one of his most helpful "smoke detector" tools was "Adding Name Tags" (from Week One). By going through his day and observing his level of stress, as well as putting a name to his emotions as they arose, Bob noticed that this increased awareness helped him to keep stress and other emotions from building up over the course of his day. Noticing that "I'm starting to feel frustrated" helped him pay more attention to what he could do in that moment to improve the situation.

Bob also recognized that sometimes his emotions became so intense so quickly that he had a tendency to fly off the handle and say or do things that he later regretted. During those times he needed to have a "fire extinguisher" tool in place. He recognized that the most important first step was to remove himself immediately from the situation. As obvious as this seemed, he often didn't do it. He decided that when he became triggered by family members, he needed to retreat to his bedroom, walk outside, or lock himself in the bathroom (whatever was closest). Once removed from the situation, he decided he would use mindful breathing until his body felt calmer.

Example: After completing this exercise Monique (from Week Six) recognized that the most essential exercises for her to maintain a sense of balance and positivity in her life involved acts of loving kindness toward herself and others. She noticed that when she did this, she seemed more resilient to her daily stressors, and noted that this was a great proactive strategy for her. After looking over her assignments from the past seven weeks, Monique found that her biggest stress triggers tended to involve times when she exploded at others with whom she didn't agree. The tool most helpful as her "fire extinguisher" was "Walking in Someone Else's Shoes," from Week Seven.

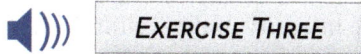 **EXERCISE THREE**

Using Mindfulness Skills to Break out of Automatic Programs

The next three exercises (Exercises Three, Four and Five) will offer you an opportunity to combine several tools to help break out of old, automatic programs that are no longer serving you.

Take some time to think about a common situation that triggers a stress response in you. If there is something currently causing you stress, you can focus on that thing, or you may want to look back over your written assignments to notice patterns and common triggers and choose one. In the following exercise, you will practice using mindfulness skills to prevent yourself from falling into automatic patterns and habitual ways of reacting. You will then practice "changing the channel" and dialing up a different emotion, thought, and behavior that might be more helpful to you. Some of this may seem familiar from previous week's chapters and that is intentional. After working on the individual skills in each chapter, you now have an opportunity to practice them further and combine some of them. Set aside about 10 minutes to do this. You may follow the script below, or follow along using the audio recording.

Take a few minutes to breathe deeply and easily, sitting upright and feeling your feet planted firmly on the ground. Allow each inhalation to be an invitation to relax more deeply, and allow each exhalation to be an invitation to release any stress and tension from your body. When you feel ready, call to mind the situation that triggers you and begin to notice your tendency to respond in habitual, automatic, and unhelpful ways. Rather than let yourself get pulled into that, take a moment to simply notice it, observing what happens in your body as you do.

Name the emotions that are present for you and see if you can sit mindfully with those emotions, allowing them to be there and continuing to breathe. It may be helpful for you to experience these emotions as you imagine yourself as a tree with deep roots going into the earth. Feel your roots, visualize them, and notice how those roots keep the tree stable and strong, even as storms pass overhead. Feel yourself grounded and stable as you stay with the sensations in your body and simply observe what is occurring.

Over time, it is likely that the intensity of the feelings will lessen. If you are able, step back and observe what is there from a wider perspective. If and when it feels right for you to do so, imagine "changing the channel." Focus on thoughts, feelings, and actions that might be helpful and that are different from your automatic response. You can view this as a kind of gentle experiment in your mind, simply trying out different thoughts, feelings, and actions, and seeing what this new "channel" is like for you.

Take some time to make this as real as possible for yourself and see the situation played out in as much detail as you can. See yourself reacting differently, observe yourself, and notice how this feels in your body. Take in any positive emotions that arise from this experience.

Example: Petra noticed that whenever her mother-in-law was around she would become easily triggered by her mother-in-law's controlling nature, and she would experience a stress response that resulted in her feeling extremely frustrated, angry, anxious, and defeated. These feelings would often last for days. Her typical response was to become anxious and retreat from the situation, becoming sullen, quiet, and angry inside. As Petra did this exercise and imagined her mother-in-law visiting, she was able to sit with her strong emotions. She became aware that what she felt in her body was very familiar, and reminded her of how she used to feel around her ex-husband, who often became quite loud, angry, and overbearing. Once she had this realization, her anxiety began to lessen. She was able to come up with a different set of thoughts focused around the fact that this was not her ex-husband but her mother-in-law, a harmless but annoying woman who visited for only short periods of time. She reminded herself that she was safe in this situation, though irritated, and she imagined calling up feelings of safety. She also saw herself taking some different actions; rather than retreating, she saw herself speaking up and setting boundaries, letting her mother-in-law know when she did things that really bothered her. She felt empowered from this exercise, and she spent some time letting those feelings soak in.

EXERCISE FOUR

Rewriting the Script

Exercise Four is a variation on the previous exercise and it offers another way to break old, unhelpful patterns of behavior using a tool of "rewriting the script."

Begin by thinking about a situation that causes you repeated stress. If possible, pick a situation different than in the previous exercise. Spend a few minutes focusing on this situation, calling it up in your mind, and noticing what story you are telling yourself about it. Imagine telling your "story" to someone else, and listen how it would sound; or, if you like, you can write it down. For example, you might start with something like "My kids are driving me crazy because they never listen to me when I ask them to do something," or "It's always such a nightmare getting to work in the morning. I waste half my day." Asking yourself the following questions can be helpful:

- What do you say to yourself about this situation? Notice if there is a "woe is me" quality, a helplessness, a lack of agency.
- What are the habitual ways that you tend to think about this situation? What negative thought traps do you fall into?
- Is your thinking all or nothing?
- Do you feel like a victim, trapped without choices?
- In what ways does your behavior reinforce your story?
- How old is this story?

Notice whether your emotions about this situation arise from your thinking or your behaviors, or both. Also, notice how the story "feeds" the emotions that you experience.

Now stop and ask yourself what is true about this story, and what is just perspective. How might you tell the story from a different perspective, or change the story to make it more helpful for you? Make sure that the new story feels accurate and true for you (e.g., don't say, "I love sitting in traffic," if that isn't the case).

Using the examples above, perhaps your new story might sound like the following: "I've noticed how frustrated I get when my kids don't do what I ask. I know they're not bad kids, but somehow my requests aren't getting through. I am going to work on trying to communicate differently and motivating them in more positive ways;" or, "Sitting in traffic tends to trigger my stress response in a major way. Instead of feeling like I'm missing out on my day, I've decided to use that time to listen to some great books on tape I've downloaded to help make my morning more enjoyable."

Go ahead and tell yourself a different story about the same circumstances. When you rewrite this story, what changes in your emotional experience and your resulting behavior? Do you feel more empowered? More hopeful? Do you make different choices? See different solutions?

Example: Danielle suffered from chronic pain after a back injury five months earlier. In doing this exercise, she realized that the story she told herself and others sounded something like this: "This pain has ruined my life. I can't do the things I used to do, and nobody understands how difficult this is." Danielle was able to recognize from this exercise that her thinking tended to be catastrophic and all or nothing. This story made her feel sorry for herself, helpless, and even bitter. Because of this repeated story, she found that she became angry towards others more easily, and even pushed people away and isolated herself frequently. She had been telling herself this story for a number of months, and she felt quite unhappy and disconnected.

In rewriting this story, Danielle knew that she needed to acknowledge her pain (both physical and emotion), but in a more compassionate and helpful way. Her rewritten story sounded something like this: "This pain has been very difficult for me, and has made me feel sad and angry that I haven't been able to do some of the things I used to love doing, such as vigorous physical activities. At the same time, I am going to work on seeing it as an opportunity to do quieter activities that I may not have had time for previously. Also, it may be an opportunity to allow others to help and support me, since I know I have many people in my life who truly care about me. I am going to make an effort to appreciate the little moments of goodness in each day so I don't get swallowed up by my anger."

In this rewritten version of her story, Danielle felt more empowered and hopeful. In fact, after doing this exercise, she decided to sign up for a painting class and discovered that this was a great creative outlet for her. By allowing others to help and support her, and by making an effort to find small things to feel grateful for, she discovered that the joy began to return to her life.

 **EXERCISE FIVE**

Practicing the Dance (Combining Multiple Skills)

Building on the previous exercises, today you have the opportunity to further practice combining multiple tools in helpful ways. This exercise will walk you through a sequence that involves sitting mindfully with a difficult emotion and anchoring yourself with breath ("dropping your anchor"), putting things in perspective and adjusting irrational thinking, and then focusing your attention on something you are grateful for. Ideally, this exercise can first be practiced as a meditation/visualization exercise, and then tried out in the course of your day as stress arises. It is best to pick something of mild to moderate intensity. I don't recommend trying this with something that is too intense or overwhelming.

To practice, set aside a small amount of time when you won't be interrupted. Follow along with the audio if you are able. Bring to mind something that is currently creating a difficult emotion for you (it could be sadness, fear, anger, frustration, irritation, etc.).

Take some time to ground yourself by dropping your imaginary anchor in the ocean floor and imagining the feelings of stability and safety that this can create. You may imagine that the emotions you are experiencing are like strong waves in the ocean. See them rise and fall around you as your ship remains steady. Allow the steady flow of your breath in and out to create a feeling of safety inside, even as you remain present with your emotions. If the feelings are intense, you might imagine them washing over you with each breath as you envision ocean waves rising and falling. Picture your feelings like those waves that come and go in the vast ocean. Stay with this step for as long as it feels right for you.

When you feel ready, imagine looking at your problem or situation through the lens of a special telescope that allows you to see the whole picture. If this situation involves upset toward another person, you might imagine "stepping into their shoes" for a few minutes. Take some time to notice your thoughts, and in particular, make note of any thoughts that seem extreme or irrational in some way. If it feels right to do so, practice replacing those thoughts with more rational or helpful ones, and notice what happens in your body and mind as you do that. Don't force this; the most important thing is simply to notice your thinking and how it may be spiraling you. Chances are, if you are mindful and present, you may begin to notice other possibilities and other ways of looking at the situation that weren't there before. If you don't, that is OK too, just continue to be present and aware of how your thinking influences your emotions.

When you feel ready, begin to call up something in your life for which you feel grateful. This is not about pushing aside whatever was bothering you, but simply shifting the focus of your attention for a moment to feelings of appreciation. As you do that, notice where you feel that positive emotion in your body, and see if you can allow that feeling to be there, and perhaps even spread throughout your body as you focus on feelings of gratitude. Stay with this feeling for as long as you like.

Before finishing this exercise, take a moment to check in with yourself by calling up the original situation and notice if anything has shifted or changed for you.

As you go through your day today, see if you might have an opportunity to practice combining several of the skills that you have learned in this book. You might pick some that work best for you, or perhaps those that you feel you most need to practice. Feel free to mix and match skills to find what is most helpful for you in different situations.

> *Example*: Asha, a primary care doctor at a busy practice and mother of three children, focused on a common challenging emotion for her: the frustration of having too little time in her day to get everything done, and feeling overwhelmed and irritable. She did this exercise in her car in the parking lot outside her office before starting her work day. Asha found it helpful to anchor herself with her breathing. She imagined her feelings of overwhelm and her anxiousness about not having enough time as waves washing up onto the shore and back out into the ocean, even as her ship remained steady and safe in the harbor. After a few minutes, she noticed some of the tension in her body eased. She imagined looking at her day and her life through a telescope where she could get some distance and

perspective. From this view, she realized she was starting her day with unhelpful thoughts, such as "I know I'll never have enough time to get everything done today . . . I never have enough time . . . I can't stand this." While there was some truth to the fact that she couldn't finish all the things she wanted to do on a given day, she realized that all of the important things seemed to get done each day. She chose to shift her thoughts slightly, to tell herself, "Even though I often have so much on my plate, I somehow manage to get everything done that I need." The tension in her shoulders relaxed a bit as she said this to herself. She decided to focus on how grateful she was for having a job where she got paid every day for helping people with their health. She called up a feeling of fulfillment in this, as well as feelings of being blessed to go home to her three children—dirty diapers, mess, and all. She was able to take this exercise into her day. Just by making a slight shift in her thinking and in the focus of her attention, she found that she felt more positive throughout her day, and less overwhelmed.

EXERCISE SIX

Finding Your Motivation Going Forward

Having the motivation to stick with something is an important part of learning new skills and making them a part of your life. For example, all of the diet and exercise books in the world won't help if you don't implement the ideas in them. Likewise, finding the motivation to practice the skills in this book is critical to your long term well-being. Today's exercise will involve self-reflection to identify what has helped in your life to motivate you to achieve success with something important to you.

Take a moment to think about something that you have successfully learned, achieved, followed through with, or created in your life that you feel good about. It could be something recent (running your first road race; learning a new software program; finishing a piece of artwork) or something from your past (learning to ride a bike, passing a major exam in school). Ask yourself these questions:

- What helped you stick with it?
- What helped motivate you to reach your goal?

- What qualities in yourself did you call upon to help you achieve success?
- What outside support did you receive, if any?
- Did you break the goal down into smaller steps? Did you need any external structure to stay on track?

Now ask yourself the following: How can I use the answers to these questions to help me put the principles in this book into practice in my life? Write down what you come up with, and use it to help assist you in the next and last assignment for this week: Exercise Seven.

Example: Ronna recalled that when her doctor told her that she needed to start exercising to stay healthy, she found it helped to pick a concrete goal to achieve to keep her motivated. For her, this was running a 5K road race. All her life, she had struggled to find the motivation to exercise, but having a measurable goal was helpful for her. Each day, she wrote down what was on her "training plan" and she put those into her phone as daily reminders. She also elicited the interest of a friend to train with her, which was a huge help to Ronna. She also posted notecards on her mirror and refrigerator to remind herself why being active was so important. Identifying what worked for her in the past gave her some ideas for how to stay motivated to practice the skills from this book. You will see how this experience influenced her action plan in the next exercise.

> **EXERCISE SEVEN**

Coming Up with Your Individualized Wellness Action Plan

In today's exercise, you will have an opportunity to develop your own individualized wellness action plan to carry you forward once you have completed this book. How will you create a healthy diet of thoughts, feelings, and behaviors in your life? As with all good diet plans, they are really not "diets" at all, but healthy lifestyle changes that are intended to continue indefinitely. There will be days when you will be successful nurturing yourself with healthy thoughts, feelings, and behaviors and other days when you are less successful, and this is normal. The important thing is that you persevere. All it takes is one small change at a time to decrease your stress and increase your sense of well-being. In order to assist yourself with this, set aside some time to review the previous exercises you have done.

Go back to the first, second, and sixth exercises in this week's chapter to help you decide what will be most helpful in your individualized wellness plan. Which skills do you most need to practice, and which ones do you already use fairly well? What proactive strategies will most help promote a sense of greater well-being in your life? What "fire extinguisher" skills can you commit to using when needed? Also, what do you already know about your own motivation and ability to work toward a goal that could help you continue to practice the skills from this book?

Take into account your learning style. Are you someone who does best working on one thing, or multiple things at a time. Take into account your lifestyle and typical day, so that you can build in a plan of action that is realistic for you. You are better off choosing a small goal that you know you can tackle rather than an action plan that requires more than you can realistically do.

Think about how you can incorporate and practice what you have learned into 10 minutes a day going forward. Also, think about what structures might be helpful to you: Are you someone who needs to write things down on a calendar to stick with something, set reminders on your phone, find a friend or partner to do things with to stay motivated or something else?

Your plan can be as simple or elaborate as you like. Know that you can reassess after a week, or a month, and append, or change anything you like. In fact, this is recommended as your needs will change over time. I recommend that you periodically revisit the self-test in Exercise One, on page 205 of this chapter, and redetermine what you most need to work on, and then revise your wellness action plan accordingly.

> *Example*: Ronna's self-test indicated that one of the areas that was most challenging for her was staying present and being in the moment. From the previous exercise, she noted that having a concrete, measurable goal was helpful, so she decided that her goal was to practice some form of mindfulness for 10 minutes a day for the next three weeks. She set her phone with a daily reminder of what she

was going to practice that day. For example, Monday was "mindfully brush teeth and take a mindful shower;" Tuesday was "go for a walk during lunch break, focusing on the sensations in my feet;" Wednesday was "sit quietly and practice following my breath for 10 minutes after work," etc. She knew that posting note cards around the house helped her to exercise daily, so she decided to leave sticky notes around the house with encouraging statements about the value of living her life in the present moment and the value of mindfulness for her well-being. In addition, because Ronna was more successful when she could practiced new skills in a group, she signed up for a local meditation class that met once a week. Ronna saw all of these as great proactive strategies to build wellness into her life.

For Ronna's "fire extinguisher" strategy, Ronna made a commitment to herself that when she began to feel overwhelmed by strong emotions or thoughts, she would listen to the "Tree with Roots" exercise she downloaded to her phone.

Example: Channah, (from Weeks Six and Seven) found that the exercises that seemed to make the most difference in helping with her depression were "Wiring in Satisfaction," "Wiring in Calm" and the "Tipping the Scale" exercise. She committed to focusing on these exercises over the next three weeks. After that, she planned to reassess her needs and modify her plan as appropriate. She knew that she did best when she wrote things down, so she made a simple chart where she could check off what she had practiced each day and write brief notes about what she noticed. For example, she noticed that on the morning when she practiced "wiring in calmness," this feeling stayed with her throughout her entire morning, and helped her manage the stress she encountered in a less reactive way.

For her "fire extinguisher," Janet agreed that whenever she started to feel her stress rising into her "red zone," she would use the "moment of hesitation" and take a few minutes to pause and be with whatever she was experiencing in a compassionate way. Because it was so hard for her to remember to use this strategy in the moment, and because she responded well to fun incentives, she decided to reward herself every time she used this skill by putting a stone in a small jar. When the jar was full, she decided to do something nurturing for herself, such as get a manicure or treat herself to her favorite healthy smoothie at the local juice bar.

Example: The following excerpts from other personal wellness plans can be used to give you some further ideas.

- For the next several weeks, I am committed to using the daily stress thermometers. When I find that my stress is going up, I will use one or more of the following to help reset my thermometer: I will set aside 3 or so minutes to pause, breathe slowly, and think about something that I am grateful for in my life, or I will imagine sending feelings of compassion to myself or someone else; I will practice the "moment of hesitation," or I will "change the radio station." My sister and I will both work on our goals independently, but check in with each other every week to share our observations and what has been helpful.

- Every day this week, I am going to replace my "have to's" with "get to's" and notice what changes and shifts for me as I do that. I am also going to set a mindfulness bell to go off on my phone every hour, and when I hear it I am going to notice whether my mind is in the past, present or future. I will gently guide my mind back to the present moment, and stay focused on my breathing for a minute.

- Over the next two weeks, whenever I have to talk with my kids about something I need them to do or something I am upset about, I am going to practice "walking in their shoes." I am also going to make a commitment to doing at least one kind act each week that I wouldn't have otherwise done and spending one night each week writing in a gratitude journal.

◀))) FINAL MEDITATION AND WRITING ACTIVITY

LEARNING WHAT WE MOST NEED IN THE MOMENT
AND PUTTING IT ALL TOGETHER

This exercise will resemble Exercise Seven in Week One, but will now allow you to incorporate everything that you have learned over these eight weeks. Set aside 10 minutes for this meditation and feel free to listen to the audio recording if you are able.

Begin by getting into a position where you can remain comfortable for about 10 minutes. Feel the pull of gravity on your body, holding you securely on the surface you are sitting or lying on. At the same time, feel your spine upright and begin to feel the breath enter your body with each inhalation. Invite your muscles to relax with each exhalation. Follow several cycles of breath, just breathing in and breathing out, to your comfortable rhythm. Invite your body to feel safe and relaxed as you return again and again to your breath.

When you are ready, imagine that you can see yourself going through your day and week. First, as you do this, see your former self and notice old patterns of stress and negativity that may be present. Notice any negative thoughts, behaviors, and emotions that tend to arise as you move through different settings. Become aware of how these negative thoughts, behaviors, and emotions no longer serve you, and note their tendency to spiral and feed off one another. Become clear of the traps that you fall into as you watch these scenes unfold. Spend as much time with this as you need, until you feel fully aware of all of the things that haven't worked for you and all the ways that you have contributed to your own unhappiness, stress, and negativity.

When you are ready, imagine changing the scenes. This time, as you go through your day and week, see yourself using all the tools that you have learned. See yourself moving through each day with greater joy, ease, and peace. Imagine encountering obstacles and stressors, and see yourself deciding what you most need to foster your own well-being in any given situation. Do you need to make space and be with a difficult emotion and bring compassion to yourself? Do you need to put your attention on another aspect of the situation, or see it differently? Do you need to shift faulty thinking? Do you need to be more present in the moment, and less in the past or future? Do you need to take some action that will help you feel better by producing a positive emotional experience? Do you need to dial up some calmness or serenity by using imagery in your mind? See yourself regulating difficult emotions and cultivating positive ones with all the tools that you have learned. Notice what you are thinking, feeling, and doing differently.

Finally, see yourself six months or one year from now, transformed and living the life you want, having learned all the tools you have been practicing and see them integrated into your life. What did you do to get to this place? What has helped you to transform your life to one of greater joy and well-being? Take some time to enjoy the abundance and positivity in your life. Stay with these positive feelings as long as you like. When you are ready, bring your attention back in to the room at your own pace.

Take some time to write down what you learned/discovered, and what you want to remember from this experience.

WEEKLY REFLECTION

♦ I am committed to setting small goals for myself to continue practicing what I have been learning. As I do this, I am undoing old, automatic patterns that no longer serve me in my life, and I am carving out new pathways in my brain toward greater well-being.

♦ I am feeding myself a healthy dose of positive thoughts, feelings, and behaviors on a regular basis to decrease my stress and enrich my life.

♦ I am becoming increasingly aware of how my thoughts and emotions can spiral me, and I am becoming increasingly adept at regulating my emotions, shifting my attention, and choosing helpful actions to experience more positivity in my life.

♦ I know that just by doing one, small thing a day, no matter how small, I am taking steps to care for myself and in turn, care for those around me.

♦ With practice, I am able to recognize what I most need in any given situation, whether it is being more present in the moment, making space for difficult emotions, recognizing unhelpful thinking, or cultivating positive experiences through my thoughts and actions.

♦ With practice, I am creating a transformation that will have lasting implications for my health, relationships, and happiness in my life.

KEY SUMMARY POINTS

- In order to make lasting changes in your life using the tools from this book, it is important to find daily ways to practice what you have learned.

- It can help to take an inventory of your strengths and areas of challenge in order to assess where you might benefit most from focusing your attention. This can be done periodically, as your needs may change over time.

- There are wonderful tools out in the world, but the only effective ones are those that you actually use.

- Learning to be comfortable with the individual skills and tools so you can combine them in different ways can be helpful for managing life's challenges with greater ease.

- Developing an individualized wellness action plan, based on your individual needs and lifestyle, is one of the most effective ways of carrying forward what you have learned over these eight weeks.

CONCLUSION

Congratulations on completing this book! You have taken important steps on your journey toward decreasing stress in your life and cultivating well-being. This is no small task, so take a moment to appreciate all of the effort that you have put into this. Also take a moment to reflect on what has changed or shifted for you since you began this program.

Please come visit my web site at BethKurland.com, where I have companion materials to help you as you continue your journey toward well-being, including free audio and video meditations, blogs to inspire well-being and more. I hope to see you there.

Warmly,

Beth

Week 8, Exercise 1 SELF-TEST		
Score (1–7) for each question:		
1a	1b	1a–1b score
2a	2b	2a–2b score
3a	3b	3a–3b score
4a	4b	4a–4b score
5a	5b	5a–5b score
6a	6b	6a–6b score
7a	7b	7a–7b score

From the above information, which chapters might you most benefit from working on further?

©2017 Beth Kurland, Ph.D.

Week 8, Exercise 2

SMOKE DETECTORS AND
FIRE EXTINGUISHERS

List "smoke detector" strategies:

List "fire extinguisher" exercises:

Describe typical situations in which you might use each of these strategies in the future:

©2017 Beth Kurland, Ph.D.

Week 8, Exercise 3

USING MINDFULNESS SKILLS TO BREAK OUT OF AUTOMATIC PROGRAMS

Observations from this meditation:

Pick a common situation that triggers stress in your day (one that you didn't use for the meditation) and write how you might use this exercise to help you cope with this stressor:

©2017 Beth Kurland, Ph.D.

Week 8, Exercise 4
REWRITING THE SCRIPT

Name a situation that causes you repeated stress:

Write out your "old script:"

Rewrite this script to be more accurate and/or helpful:

What changes in your emotional experience and resulting behavior by rewriting your script? Do you feel more empowered? More hopeful? Do you make different choices? See different solutions?

©2017 Beth Kurland, Ph.D.

Week 8, Exercise 5
PRACTICING THE DANCE
(Combining Multiple Skills)

Observations from the meditation exercise:

Write down any ways you were able to combine several skills from this book in your day today.

Week 8, Exercise 6
FINDING YOUR MOTIVATION GOING FORWARD

Name something that you have accomplished or achieved in your life (large or small) that you feel good about:

Ask yourself the following questions and write down your responses:

What helped you stick with it?

What helped motivate you to reach your goal?

What qualities in yourself did you call upon to help you achieve success?

What outside support did you receive, if any?

Did you break the goal down into smaller steps?

Did you use any external support to stay on track?

Now write down how you can use the answers to these questions to help you put the principles in this book into practice:

©2017 Beth Kurland, Ph.D.

Week 8, Exercise 7
COMING UP WITH YOUR INDIVIDUALIZED WELLNESS ACTION PLAN

Review the previous exercises from Week 8, and from previous weeks if you want. Use your responses from exercises 1, 2 and 6 of Week 8 especially, to help decide which strategies will be most helpful in your individualized wellness plan.

Write out your personal wellness plan here:.

©2017 Beth Kurland, Ph.D.

Week 8, Final Meditation and Writing Activity

 LEARNING WHAT WE MOST NEED IN THE MOMENT AND PUTTING IT ALL TOGETHER

After doing the meditation, write out your answer to the following:

See yourself six months or one year from now, transformed and living the life you want, having learned all the tools you have been practicing and seeing them integrated into your life. What did you do to get to this place? What has helped you to transform your life to one of greater joy and well-being?

Write down what you have learned/discovered from this meditation exercise.

©2017 Beth Kurland, Ph.D.

REFERENCES

American Psychological Association. (2012, January 11). *Stress in America: Our health at risk*. Washington, DC: Author. Retrieved from https://www.apa.org/news/press/releases/stress/2011/final-2011.pdf

Begley, S. (2008). *Train you mind change your brain*. New York, NY: Ballentine Books.

Benson, H., & Klipper, M. (2000). *The relaxation response*. New York, NY: HarperTorch.

Benson, H. & Proctor, W. (2010). *Relaxation Revolution: Enhancing your personal health through the science and genetics of mind body healing*. New York, NY: Scribner.

Brooks, R.B. & Goldstein, S. (2002). *Raising resilient children: Fostering strength, hope, and optimism in your child*. Lincolnwood, IL: Contemporary Books.

Childre, D.L.,& Martin, H. (1999). *The HeartMath Solution*. San Francisco, CA: HarperSanFrancisco.

Childre, D.L. & Rozman, D. (2005). *Transforming stress: the HeartMath solution for relieving worry, fatigue, and tension*. Oakland, CA: New Harbinger Publications.

Clear, J. (2013). How to be thankful for your life by changing just one word. Retrieved from http://jamesclear.com/how-to-be-thankful

Cook, C. (2014). Becoming a resilient person: The science of stress management and promoting well-being [online course]. Retrieved from https://www.edx.org/course/becoming-resilient-person-science-stress-uwashingtonx-ecfs311x-0

Davidson, R. J. (2014, July 8). Life ed: Making meditation part of daily life [Interview with Maria Shriver on NBC News]. Retrieved from http://www.nbcnews.com/feature/maria-shriver/life-ed-making-meditation-part-daily-life-n150701

Fowler, K. (2014). Putting cognitive-behavioral therapy to work for you: Combat depression, anxiety, and other problems. Retrieved from: http://athealth.com/topics/putting-cognitive-behavioral-therapy-to-work-for-you-combat-depression-anxiety-and-other-problems/

Fredrickson, B. (2009). *Positivity*. New York, NY: Crown Publishers.

Goleman, D. (1995). *Emotional intelligence: Why it can matter more than IQ*. New York, NY: Bantam Books.

Goyal, M., Singh, S., Sibinga, E. M. S., Gould, N., Rowland-Seymour, A., Sharma, R… Hay-thornthwaite, J. A. (2014). Meditation programs for psychological stress and well-being. JAMA Internal Medicine, 174(3), 357-368. doi:10.1001/jamainternmed.2013.13018

Greenspan, M. (2003). *Healing through the dark emotions: The wisdom of grief, fear, and despair.* Boston, MA: Shambhala Publications.

Hanson, R. (2011*). Just one thing: Developing a Buddha brain one simple practice at a time.* Oakland, CA: New Harbinger Publications.

Hanson, R. (2013*). Hardwiring happiness: The new brain science of contentment, calm and confidence.* New York, NY: Harmony Books.

Hanson, R. (2014-2015). The foundations of well-being: growing the good in your brain and your life [online program]. Retrieved from https://www.thefoundationsofwellbeing.com.

Hanson, R., & Mendius, R.(2009*). Buddha's brain: The practical neuroscience of happiness, love & wisdom.* Oakland, CA: New Harbinger Publications.

Harris, R. (2013). Getting unstuck in ACT: A clinician's guide to overcoming common ob-stacles in Acceptance and Commitment Therapy. Oakland, CA: New Harbinger Publica-tions.

Hayes, S.C. & Smith, S. (2005). *Get out of your mind & into your life: The new acceptance and commitment therapy.* Oakland, CA: New Harbinger Publications

Hayes, S.C., Strosahl, K.D., & Wilson K.G. (1999). *Acceptance and commitment therapy: An experiential approach to behavior change.* New York, NY: The Guilford Press.

HeartMath Institute. (n.d.). Researching the human heart and brain. Retrieved from https://www.heartmath.org/research/

Hyatt, M. (2016, Feb. 26). How a small shift in your vocabulary can instantly change your attitude: 3 suggestions to boost your mood and improve your performance. Retrieved from https://michaelhyatt.com/how-a-shift-in-your-vocabulary-can-instantly-change-your-attitude.html

Kabat-Zinn, J. (1994). *Wherever you go there you are: Mindfulness meditation in everyday life.* New York, NY: Hyperion.

Kalia, M. (2002). Assessing the economic impact of stress-the modern day hidden epidemic. *Metabolism, 51*(6 suppl 1), 49-53.

Koch, K. (2014, Dec. 1). Tone check: Converting "have-to's" into "get-to's". Retrieved from http://drkathykoch.com/tone-check-have-get/

Luoma, J.B., Hayes, S.C., and Walser, R.D. (2007). *Learning ACT: An acceptance & commitment therapy skills training manual for therapists*. Oakland, CA: New Harbinger Publications.

Lyubomirsky, S. (2008). *The how of happiness: A new approach to getting the life you want*. New York, NY: Penguin Press.

National Institute of Mental Health. (n.d.). Fact sheet on stress. Retrieved from https://www.nimh.nih.gov/health/publications/stress/index.shtml

Pasinksi, M., & Gould, J. (2011). *Beautiful brain, beautiful you: Look radiant from the inside out by empowering your mind*. New York, NY: Hyperion.

Rankin, L. (2013). *Mind over medicine: Scientific proof that you can heal yourself*. Calsbad, Calif.: Hay House.

Ricard, M., Lutz, A., & Davidson, R. (2014). Mind of the Meditator: Contemplative practices that extend back thousands of years show a multitude of benefits for both body and mind. *Scientific American*, 311(5), 38-45.

Robinson, J. (2013, May 22). Three-quarters of your doctor bills are because of this. [Blog]. Retrieved from http://www.huffingtonpost.com/joe-robinson/stress-and-health_b_3313606.html

Sapolsky, R. (1994). *Why zebras don't get ulcers: A guide to stress, stress related diseases, and coping*. New York, NY: W.H. Freeman & Company.

Seligman, M. (2006). *Learned optimism: How to change your mind and your life*. New York, NY: Vintage Books.

Siegel, R.D. (2010). *The mindfulness solution: Everyday practices for everyday problems*. New York, NY: The Guilford Press.

Siegel, R.D. (2013). Mindfulness and Psychotherapy [online program]. Retrieved from http://www.nicabm.com/mindfulnessandpsychotherapy2013/b2-info/

INDEX

H

I

J

K

L

ABOUT THE AUTHOR

Beth Kurland, Ph.D., is a licensed clinical psychologist who has been in practice since 1994, working with people across the lifespan from preschoolers through adults. With a particular passion for and expertise in mindfulness and the mind-body connection, she specializes in using mind-body strategies to help people achieve whole-person health and wellness.

Dr. Kurland graduated from Amherst College, received her doctorate from Clark University, and completed an internship at McLean Hospital and two post-doctoral fellowships, affiliated with Massachusetts General Hospital and Children's Hospital in Boston. She currently has an outpatient practice in Norwood, Massachusetts.

Beth brings over 20 years of experience in helping others achieve well-being in their lives, and invites her readers to learn and experience the strategies she has found to be most beneficial for transformation. On her website, readers can find specific companion materials to her book, including audio meditations and printable worksheets from this book, that allow readers an opportunity to more fully incorporate the strategies from this book into their daily lives.

Look for additional books by Dr. Kurland, including three children's books, each with accompanying games, to help young children learn how to cope with difficult emotions and develop greater positivity (anticipated release: 2017-2018).

For information, access to audios and worksheets plus more please visit Beth's website:
BethKurland.com

WellBridge Books™ *is an imprint of Six Degrees Publishing Group*™
WellBridgeBooks.com

CPSIA information can be obtained
at www.ICGtesting.com
Printed in the USA
BVOW07s0341160917
495019BV00004B/54/P